52 Programs for Kid

AROUND the YEAR
in Children's Church

Lisa Flinn and Barbara Younger

Abingdon Press
Nashville

Scripture quotations, unless noted otherwise, are from the Common English Bible. Copyright © 2011 by the Common English Bible. All rights reserved. Used by permission. (www.CommonEnglishBible.com)

Art Credits—page 7, 11, 22, 33, 43, 45, 51, 63, 66, 76, 86, 96, 110, 114 by Shutterstock
page 8, 15, 17, 26, 31, 34, 46, 49, 52, 57, 59, 71, 80, 83, 84, 87, 91, 95, 98, 114 by Brenda Gilliam
page 43 by Barbara Ball
page 63 by Megan Jeffery

ISBN 9781-426-74147-0

12 13 14 15 16 17 - 10 9 8 7 6 5 4 3

Manufactured in the United States of America

To Bob and Mae Lee Brizendine,
who grace Hillsborough Presbyterian Church
with their wisdom and exuberance

Table of Contents

God's Garden

Water Wonder

Color Joy

Worship Spirit

Fall Faith

Introduction

Welcome to *Around the Year in Children's Church*!

The celebration of the Christian calendar adds spiritual meaning and depth to our lives. Children embrace holy days, holidays, and the seasons with energy and enthusiasm, and they are ready and willing to learn more. These creative programs are designed to invite their attention and curiosity; engage them in the Bible, stories, conversation, music, and prayers; and guide them in fun, faith-building games and crafts.

As a leader and teacher, you'll appreciate the unique ways to introduce the topic each week, the variety of approaches to storytelling, the inclusion of choices of activities in each program, and the simple list of supplies.

Thank you for using *Around the Year in Children's Church* as you share your own spiritual gifts, your time, and your talents with God's children!

We are delighted that Abingdon Press asked us to write this, our fifth children's church book.

Lisa Flinn and Barbara Younger
Hillsborough, North Carolina

Before You Get Started:

- Because the dates for some holidays such as Easter and Thanksgiving vary, you'll need to make adjustments to the order in which you use the programs. Three sections—Water Wonder, Color Joy, and Worship Spirit—are not tied to the calendar, so those programs work especially well at any time of the year.

- Basic Supplies

crayons	#4 cone coffee filters
4 x 6–inch index cards	fluted white paper plates
white copy paper	construction paper in a variety of colors
manila folders	chenille stems
glue	stapler and extra staples
scissors	tape
hole punch	yarn or ribbon

- Crayons are preferred over markers for coloring because they don't stain fingers or clothes and they won't dry out. However, if you are making something that will be sent through the mail, such as postcards, or will be sent through a copy machine, such as a bulletin cover, markers are preferable, as they will not melt when running through a hot machine.

- Recruit a helper each week. Don't overlook teens in your congregation, who are great role models for younger kids.

- If serving snacks, be aware of food allergies.

Advent and Christmas Adventure

Mary and the Angel

Message:
God chose Mary to be the mother of Jesus.

Greeting with a Gift Bag
Locate a representation of Mary from a Nativity set, greeting card, or story illustration. Place it in a gift bag.

Greet the children. Hold up the gift bag. Choose a child to reach into the bag and discover what's inside. Have the child show the group.

Ask: Who do you think this person might be? Why is Mary special?

Say: God chose Mary to be the mother of Jesus. We don't know exactly how Mary looked because she lived long ago, but artists use their imaginations to help us understand that she was a real person.

Getting Set for the Story
Say: Mary was chosen by God to be the mother of Jesus. Let's hear the Bible story written in the book of Luke.

Say: You will play a listening game as I read. There are three special words you'll hear over and over. When you hear "God," point to heaven. When you hear "angel," flap your hands at ear level. When you hear "Mary," fold your hands in prayer.

Demonstrate the motions, and then say the words as the children practice each one.

Telling the Story
Say: GOD sent the ANGEL Gabriel to a city in Galilee called Nazareth. In Nazareth, there lived a young woman named MARY. MARY was engaged to be married to Joseph. Joseph's family was related to the famous king David, who had lived a long time before them.

When the ANGEL came to MARY, he brought a message from GOD. "Rejoice, favored one!" said the ANGEL to MARY. "The Lord is with you!"

MARY was surprised to see an ANGEL, and she was confused by his message. MARY wondered what sort of greeting the ANGEL had given her.

Bible Verse
When the angel came to her, he said, "Rejoice, favored one! The Lord is with you!" (Luke 1:28)

Supplies
- Representation of Mary
- Holiday gift bag

The ANGEL understood MARY'S feelings. He said, "Do not be afraid. GOD is honoring you. You will have a baby boy. You will call him Jesus. He will be great and the Son of the Most High."

Then MARY said, "I am the Lord's servant. Let it be with me just as you have said." After hearing MARY's answer, the ANGEL left her.

Exploring

Make Good News Angels to remember Gabriel's visit to Mary. You'll need two coffee filters for each angel.

Before Children's Church, trace and cut two inch circles from paper for the angels' heads. Also, for each angel, open a filter by gently pulling on the crimped side and bottom, resulting in a flat semi-circle. These will be the wings. Finally, for each angel, from another filter, cut off the crimped narrow bottom. This will be the angel's gown.

Make a sample Good News Angel to show the children. Scrunch the wings in the center. Wrap a strip of tape around the gathers. Open up the angel's gown with the long crimped seam down the back, and tape the wings to the top (on the crimped seam).

To complete the angel, draw a face on the paper circle. Attach the face to the front of the gown.

Say: Meet my Good News Angel!

Guide the children through the steps. If you wish, let the children color the angel's gown. Glitter glue may be used to create a halo or decorate the angel's wings or gown. Have the children put their names or initials on their angels.

Invite everyone to hold her or his Good News Angel and say, "Rejoice, favored one!"

Say: "Rejoice, favored one!" means "Be joyful. You are special."

Ask: Why was Mary special?

Say: God chose Mary to be the mother of Jesus. The angel told Mary that God loved her and that her baby would be holy. Mary was happy to receive this good news.

Set the Good News Angels aside.

Celebrating with Music

Teach the children the first verse of "To a Maid Engaged to Joseph" by playing a recording or singing the song for them. This Christmas carol is available on CDs and is included in many hymnals.

More Exploring

The children will be messengers in the Names of Jesus Game as they take turns declaring the names given to Jesus.

Before Children's Church, print each of these names on a separate card:

Wonderful Counselor (Isaiah 9:6)

Mighty God (Isaiah 9:6)

Eternal Father (Isaiah 9:6)

Prince of Peace (Isaiah 9:6)

Jesus (Luke 1:31)

Son of the Most High (Luke 1:32)

Christ (Matthew 1:16)

Alpha and Omega (Revelation 1:8)

Good Shepherd (John 10:14)

King of Kings (Revelation 19:16)

Lord of Lords (Revelation 19:16)

Emmanuel (Matthew 1:23)

Savior (Titus 3:6)

The Word (John 1:1)

You'll need two containers. Put the Names of Jesus cards into one of them.

When it's time to play the game, place the container holding the names at one end of the room. Have the children line up by that container. You will stand at the other end of the room with the empty container.

Say: In our Bible story, Mary was told to name her baby Jesus. The name Jesus means "He will save his people." The people who recorded God's word in the Bible also used more names to describe who Jesus was and what he did.

Say: Let's play the Names of Jesus Game! You are messengers and will each take a turn picking a name card from the container. When it's your turn, bring the Names of Jesus card to me. I will say, "Thank you, messenger! This card says . . . Will you please announce the name to the group?" Then you will say, "Hail, favored ones! The baby's name is ____."

Recycle the cards back into the container to accommodate all the children or to play the game again. Conclude by reading all of the Names of Jesus cards.

Say: The angel Gabriel was a messenger from God. Today you've been messengers for Jesus, proclaiming his many names!

Bonus Activity

Art books, Christmas books, or children's Bibles often have illustrations of Mary and angels. Bookmark these illustrations to share with the children. As you show each one, tell the children the title of the work of art and the artist, when given. Encourage comments and questions.

Saying Goodbye

Give the children their Good News Angels. Hand out the Names of Jesus cards if you wish.

Say: The Advent season begins with the angel Gabriel bringing a message to Mary. God chose Mary to be the mother of Jesus. Rejoice!

Note

If you have children who can read, encourage them to read the name for themselves. Remind the children that "Hail, favored ones!" means "Be happy! You are special!"

Supplies

- Books with illustrations of Mary and angels
- Bookmarks

Bible Verse
She will give birth to a son, and you will call him Jesus. (Matthew 1:21)

Supplies
- Representation of Mary from last week
- Representation of Joseph
- Holiday gift bag

Supplies
- Headscarf or fabric and something to tie it with (optional)

Pray
Holy God, thank you for sending Jesus to tell us that you love us. Thank you for Joseph and Mary, who helped Jesus to grow. Help us to know that you love and care for us. Amen.

Supplies
- Plain manila folders
- Paper
- Crayons

Joseph Has a Dream

Message:
Joseph believed in God's plan.

Greeting with a Gift Bag
Locate a representation of Joseph from a Nativity set, greeting card, or story illustration. Place it in the gift bag. Have the representation of Mary from last week visible. Greet the children. Hold up the gift bag. Invite them, one by one, to gently squeeze the bag.

Choose a child to reach into the bag and pull out what's inside. Have the child show the group. Place the representation of Joseph next to that of Mary.

Getting Set for the Story
Lead the story in the character of Joseph. To set the scene, consider wearing a headscarf as Joseph did. A scarf or a piece of fabric tied with ribbon, rope, or a sash will work well.

Ask: Do you remember some of your dreams?

Say: Hold up your hand if you have happy dreams. Silly dreams. Scary dreams. Dreams about your friends and family.

In today's Christmas story, we'll hear about a man who has an important and holy dream.

Telling the Story
Greetings to you! My name is Joseph, and I am a carpenter. My home and my workshop are in the city of Nazareth. I enjoy making useful and beautiful things with my hands and with tools.

I earn enough money to support a family, so I asked Mary's family if we could be married. Mary is lovely, energetic, sweet-natured, and skillful. She will be a fine wife.

But let me tell you about a dream I had last night. As I slept, an angel came to me and said, "Joseph, Son of David, I bring you good news! Mary will have a baby, and you will call him Jesus. He will be special because he will tell all the people that God loves them."

I am so happy! Mary will have a special baby sent from God. I will help Mary raise this baby and he will do great things. I will love and protect this holy baby.

Please excuse me. I must go see Mary right away. We are going to get married!

Exploring
Children will remember Joseph's dream and their own dreams with Dream Folders.

Say: The angel told Joseph to not be afraid and to take Mary as his wife. The angel also explained that a holy baby would be born and that Joseph should name him Jesus.

Give each child a manila folder.

Say: On the front of your folder, draw Joseph's dream as you imagine it.

Set out crayons. Prompt the children by recounting parts of the story. Have them write their names on the front of their folders.

After the drawings are finished, ask each child to describe her or his dream picture.

Say: Some people like to write down their dreams. They keep a dream journal. They read the journals later and think about their dreams. This folder will now become your own dream journal! You can draw pictures of your dreams and keep them in your Dream Folder.

Give each child three sheets of paper to put in the folder. Set the Dream Folders aside.

Celebrating with Music
Teach children "Jesus Is a Gift from God," set to the tune of "Mary Had a Little Lamb."

More Exploring
Play the Messengers and Dreamers Game. Divide the children into two groups. If you have an uneven number, you can fill in as a player. Assign one group to be the Messengers and the other to be the Dreamers. Place the Messengers opposite the Dreamers, in two lines facing one another, as far apart as possible.

Say: In our Messengers and Dreamers Game, each of you will have two turns as the angel bringing a message and two turns as Joseph hearing the message in a dream.

Explain that the Messengers are to fly to the Dreamers across from them and whisper the message you will give them. Say each message softly to the Messengers just before they deliver it.

• **Message One:** I have good news.

• **Message Two:** Mary will have a baby.

Next, have the groups switch roles so the Dreamers are now the Messengers and vice versa.

• **Message Three:** You will name him "Jesus."

• **Message Four:** He will tell about God's love.

When the game is finished, ask the children to repeat all four messages.

Say: Very good! We can tell the good news.

Bonus Activity
Let children use their Dream Folders to draw one of their own dreams. As the children finish, ask them to explain their drawings.

Saying Goodbye
Give the children their Dream Folders.

Say: God sent an angel to Joseph in a dream. The angel told Joseph about the coming of Jesus as a baby. Joseph loved God and promised to help Mary by being a good parent to Jesus.

Jesus is a gift from God,
gift from God, gift from God.
Jesus is a gift from God
born on Christmas Day.

Joseph . . . went up from the city of Nazareth in Galilee to . . . Bethlehem. (Luke 2:4)

Supplies

- Bible
- Representations of Mary and Joseph from previous weeks
- Representation of a donkey
- Holiday gift bag

Bethlehem Bound

Message:
Jesus will be born in Bethlehem.

Greeting with a Gift Bag
Locate a representation of a donkey from a Nativity set, greeting card, or story illustration. Place it in the gift bag. Have the representations of Mary and Joseph from the past two weeks visible. Greet the children. Hold up the gift bag. Choose a child to reach into the bag and discover what's inside. Have the child show the donkey to the group.

Open the Bible and read aloud Luke 2:1-5.

Ask: When you take a trip to the store, to school, to church, or to visit friends and family, how do you get there?

Say: In Mary and Joseph's time, there were no cars, buses, subways, bicycles, skateboards, motorcycles, or airplanes. In those days there were carts and chariots pulled by animals, horses and donkeys to be ridden, and a variety of boats to cross water. Often people just used their feet to walk where they wanted to go. In today's story, we'll imagine what it was like for Mary and Joseph to travel to Bethlehem with the help of a donkey.

Say: While I tell the story, let's act it out.

Instruct the children to walk in place, or to follow you from room to room as you tell the story, pantomiming the actions that Mary and Joseph did.

Telling the Story
Early one morning, Joseph loaded clothes, blankets, and other supplies onto his donkey's back. At her home, Mary packed food and drink for them. *(Pantomime packing.)*

Joseph's neighbors waved and said, "Go with God" as he rode the donkey to meet Mary. Mary got on the donkey and waved goodbye to her friends. "Go with God," they called. *(Wave to your friends.)*

As the sun rose over the rooftops, Mary and Joseph left Nazareth and walked for miles. *(Walk, walk, walk.)* At lunch, they rested on a hilltop. *(Eat lunch.)*

That afternoon, Mary rode the donkey for hours and hours until they came to the home of Joseph's relatives. *(Walk, walk, walk.)* After supper, they said their prayers and slept. *(Pray, then sleep.)*

The next day, Joseph and Mary walked and walked. *(Walk, walk, walk.)* In the afternoon, Mary rode the donkey, but she felt so tired that Joseph stopped and made camp for the night. They thanked God for one another and fell asleep. *(Pray, then sleep.)*

As they began a new day on the road, Mary and Joseph saw many other travelers. People going the same way chatted, and they waved to those they knew. *(Wave at your friends.)* Mary and Joseph walked for hours. *(Walk, walk, walk.)* At nightfall, they prayed and then slept in an olive grove among other travelers. *(Pray, then sleep.)*

Later the next morning, *(Walk, walk, walk.)* Mary and Joseph stopped at a well for fresh water. *(Drink from your hands.)* After hours on the road, they found a guesthouse and thanked God. *(Pray, then sleep.)*

The following morning, Mary and Joseph had to wait as several shepherds and their flocks crossed the road. *(Stop and tap foot.)* After walking for many more miles *(Walk, walk, walk.)*, Joseph's sandal strap broke, so he took another pair from his pack. *(Put on sandal.)* That night they took the last room in the guesthouse, said their prayers, and slept. *(Pray, then sleep.)*

On the next day, the donkey was acting stubborn. Mary coaxed him with some treats. *(Pretend to give the donkey treats.)* She knew the donkey was tired, too. They went on, hour after hour, mile after mile. *(Walk, walk, walk.)* Finally, they found a guesthouse. *(Pray, then sleep.)*

The following day was difficult. *(Walk, walk, walk.)* The roads were especially crowded. Late in the afternoon, Mary needed to stop. *(Stop walking.)* A woman passing by saw that Mary was expecting a baby and invited Mary and Joseph to stay the night at her home. *(Pray, then sleep.)*

The next day, as they came near the big city of Jerusalem, the crowds were huge. They stopped at a guesthouse earlier than usual, offered evening prayers, and then they slept. *(Pray, then sleep.)*

Mary and Joseph left at daybreak, determined to reach the city of Bethlehem. *(Walk, walk, walk.)* They traveled all morning and all afternoon. As the sun sank low in the sky, they came in to Bethlehem. Mary and Joseph praised God that they had arrived safely. They knew the baby Jesus would be born here in Bethlehem.

Exploring
Make Go with God Greeting Cards. If you use photocopied maps, invite the children to color a dot on Nazareth and one on Bethlehem. Have them draw a line between the two cities. Next, ask them to fold the paper in half, so the map is on the inside. Have them print "Go with God" on the front of the card and then decorate the card with drawings, and foil star stickers if available.

For plain paper, fold the paper in half. Have the children write "Go with God" on the front. Suggest they draw vehicles used for travel on the inside, such as cars, boats, subways, planes, and bicycles. Add foil star stickers if available.

Celebrating with Music
Teach children "We Must Go to Bethlehem," set to the tune of "Mary Had a Little Lamb." You may also want to sing the beloved Christmas carol, "Oh Little Town of Bethlehem."

Bonus Activity
Let the children play Pin the Tail on the Donkey! This game is sold in the party section at many stores.

Saying Goodbye
Give the children their Go with God Greeting Cards to present to others.

Say: Bethlehem is where Jesus was born. Soon we'll celebrate his birthday!

We must go to Bethlehem,
Bethlehem, Bethlehem.
We must go to Bethlehem,
walking down the road.
Baby Jesus will be born,
will be born, will be born.
Baby Jesus will be born,
born in Bethlehem.

Supplies

- Representations of Mary, Joseph, Baby Jesus, the manger, and stable animals
- Holiday gift bag

Supplies

- Figurines of Mary, Joseph, Baby Jesus, the manger, and stable animals
- Stable (optional)

Note

You may need to change the animal sounds to match the figurines you have available.

Jesus Is Born!

Message:

Jesus, our Savior, is born!

Greeting with a Gift Bag

Locate figures from a Nativity set, greeting card, or story illustration. Place the items in the gift bag.

Greet the children. Hold up the gift bag. Choose one or several children to reach into the gift bag to discover what's inside. Have them show the group. Have the children identify the figures. Read the Bible verse.

Say: Jesus was born in a stable because there wasn't room in the guesthouse. That's why his first bed was a manger.

Getting Set for the Story

If you aren't able to locate figurines or a stable, bring an illustration from a greeting card or storybook to show the children.

Invite the children to place the manger in the center of a table. If you have a stable, place it center stage. If using an illustration, pass it around the group so everyone can have a close look.

Ask: Do you know the sounds these animals make?

Say: For our story today, we'll say "moo-moo" for the cow, "hee-haw" for the donkey, "bah-bah" for the sheep, and "coo-coo" for the dove. Let's practice!

Lead the children in practicing the sounds when you say the name of each animal.

Telling the Story

After traveling all day, Mary and Joseph were very tired when they reached the city of Bethlehem. Joseph knocked on the door of the first guesthouse he saw. "We have no room," came the answer.

Going down a different street, Joseph knocked on another guesthouse door. "We have no room!" came a shout.

Again and again, he knocked on doors, trying to find a place for the night. The answer was always the same: "We have no room."

Finally, Joseph saw a lamp glowing by a wide front door. Once again, he knocked. "Sir, we have traveled far today, like so many others. We need to find a place for Mary to rest. She is expecting a baby very soon. I am worried about her. Can you help us?"

A man with a kind face said, "We don't have any place inside, but I have an idea. Behind the guesthouse, there is a stable. It's clean and there is fresh hay to rest on. The animals inside are friendly and keep the stable warm. Do you want to stay in the stable?"

"Yes," Joseph answered. "We thank you for your kindness."

Joseph brought the DONKEY (hee-haw) into the stable and helped Mary get down. Joseph then led the tired DONKEY (hee-haw) to a water trough and a manger of hay. *(Place Mary, Joseph, and the donkey in the Nativity scene.)*

The COW (moo-moo), the SHEEP (bah-bah), and the DOVE (coo-coo) greeted the visitors who were preparing to have a baby. *(Place these creatures in the Nativity scene.)*

Hours passed and the animals kept watch. When Mary finally held her newborn, the animals softly sang a stable lullaby. The COW (moo-moo), the SHEEP (bah-bah), the DONKEY (hee-haw), and the DOVE (coo-coo) all joined together to welcome the baby. *(Place Jesus in the manger.)*

The animals continued their stable lullaby as Mary cradled Jesus and Joseph made a bed for him in a manger. The COW sang (moo-moo), the SHEEP sang (bah-bah), the DONKEY sang (hee-haw), and the DOVE sang (coo-coo), because they realized this baby was holy. Mary and Joseph smiled as they placed Jesus in the sweet golden hay of the manger.

Exploring
Build Stable Nativity Scenes with a paper stable and a Nativity sticker set. If you can't locate Nativity stickers, children can draw the stable scene.

Prepare the stables. Orient the paper horizontally. Measure two inches from the top to make a horizontal line across the paper. Next, measure two inches in from the right and the left and make a vertical line on both sides.

Fold each of the lined edges toward the center of the sheet of paper. The folded sides will overlap in the top two corners. Crease firmly, and then open the folds.

The long flap will become the roof of the stable. Create a tab at each end of the roof, so it will attach easily to the sides. To do this, make a cut from the edge of the short side along the fold line (parallel with the top of the roof) until you reach the intersection of the folds.

Fold each roof tab over the side. Glue or tape the tabs. The stable is finished!

Lead the children through any steps needed to finish the stables. Next, invite them to use the Nativity sticker sets or crayons to complete their Nativity scenes. Ask them put their name or initials on the stable.

Celebrating with Music
Teach children "Away in a Manger" by playing a recording or singing the song for them.

Bonus Activity
Sing more favorite Christmas carols and/or read picture books based on the Christmas story, such as Cynthia Cotten's *This Is the Stable*, Lisa Flinn and Barbara Younger's *Unwrapping the Christmas Creche*, and Joseph Slate's *Who Is Coming to Our House?*

Saying Goodbye
Give the children their Stable Nativity Scenes.

Say: We celebrate the birth of Jesus with prayers, songs, pageants, stories, decorations, cards, and gifts. Let's remember that Jesus is a gift from God, sent to be our Savior.

Pray
Holy God, we praise you for sending us Baby Jesus. We know that when he grows up, he will preach, teach, and lead us in our faith. Amen.

Supplies
- Nativity sticker sets or crayons
- Construction paper
- Ruler
- Pencil
- Scissors
- Glue or tape

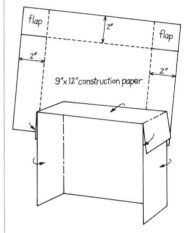

flap — 2" — flap
2" — 2"
9" x 12" construction paper

Away in a manger, no crib for a bed,
The little Lord Jesus laid down his sweet head.
The stars in the sky looked down where he lay,
The little Lord Jesus, asleep on the hay.

The angel said, "Don't be afraid! Look! I bring good news to you—wonderful, joyous news for all people." (Luke 2:10)

Supplies

- Representations of Mary, Joseph, Baby Jesus, and stable animals from previous weeks
- Representations of shepherds and sheep
- Holiday gift bag

Pray

Holy God, like the shepherds, we praise you and thank you for the good news of the birth of Jesus. He is our Savior, Christ the Lord. Amen.

Shepherds Hear Good News

Message:
Angels and shepherds told the good news of Jesus' birth.

Greeting with a Gift Bag
Have the representations of Mary, Joseph, Baby Jesus, and the animals visible. Place representations of shepherds and sheep in the gift bag.

Greet the children. Choose a child to reach into the bag and discover what is inside.

Getting Set for the Story
Say: Today, you're going to pretend you're important characters in our story. You're the shepherds! Shepherds watch over their flocks of sheep day and night. In the story of the birth of Jesus, shepherds are awake at night watching their flocks.

Tell the children that every time they hear the word "shepherds" in the story, they are to pump an arm in the air and shout out, "Yes! We're shepherds!" Practice this a few times and begin.

Telling the Story
In the fields outside the city of Bethlehem, there were SHEPHERDS guarding their sheep. It was night, and out of the darkness appeared an angel of the Lord. The angel stood before the SHEPHERDS, and the glory of the Lord shined all around. The SHEPHERDS were terrified.

The angel said, "Don't be afraid! Look! I bring good news to you—wonderful, joyous news for all people. Your Savior is born today in David's city. He is Christ the Lord."

The angel continued, "This is a sign for you: You will find a newborn baby wrapped snugly and lying in a manger."

As the SHEPHERDS listened to the angel's good news, suddenly there was a great assembly of angels saying, "Glory to God in heaven, and on earth peace among those whom he favors."

After the angels returned to heaven, the SHEPHERDS said, "Let's go right now to Bethlehem and see what's happened. We must locate the baby the Lord's angels have told us to find."

The SHEPHERDS went quickly into Bethlehem and found Mary and Joseph. Then they saw a baby lying in a manger.

When the SHEPHERDS saw the sign the angel had spoken about, they told Mary and Joseph and everyone else they met about the angel's words to them. The baby was their Savior, Christ the Lord.

All who heard this good news were amazed. Mary remembered everything the SHEPHERDS said about the angel's good news. Her baby was a Savior, Christ the Lord.

Then the SHEPHERDS returned to their sheep, praising God for the visit from the angels and for the good news of that amazing night.

Exploring

Celebrate the Christmas shepherds with Christmas Shepherd Puppets.

Prepare the puppets ahead of time. Cut a two-inch round head for each puppet. Then prepare the puppet bodies. Place the construction paper horizontally in front of you. Fold the paper into fourths. Crease the folds. Draw a line horizontally across the middle of the paper.

Next, open the paper. Cut across the pencil line to the first fold on each side.

Fold in the bottom flaps. The paper will have a T shape. Next, tape the bottom folded portion closed, so a child's fingers can slip inside.

Place the puppet body in front of the children with the bar of the T at the top and the folds of the bottom facing up. Have the children color stripes on the T. These are the sleeves of the shepherd's robe.

Turn the puppet body over. Fold the sleeves downward diagonally. Finally, have the children color a face onto the head. Tape the head onto the body.

When they are finished, let the shepherds talk to one another about the night that Jesus was born.

Celebrating with Music

Teach children "Go Tell It on the Mountain" by playing a recording or singing the song for them.

More Exploring

Repeat the angel's words in a Good News Round Robin Game.

Form a circle. Whisper a part of the angel's message to the child next to you, who will repeat it to the next child. After the good news travels around the circle back to you, repeat the message and start a new one.

Here are the messages:

1. I bring good news to you!
2. Wonderful, joyous news for all people.
3. Your Savior is born.
4. He is Christ the Lord.
5. This is a sign for you.
6. You will find him lying in a manger.
7. Glory to God in heaven.
8. Peace on earth.

Say: The angels told the good news of Jesus' birth. As Christians, we tell others too!

Bonus Activity

Treat children to a candy cane, first created in honor of the Christmas shepherds. As they enjoy the treat, read them the Twenty-third Psalm.

Saying Goodbye

Give the children their Christmas Shepherd Puppets.

Say: Angels and shepherds told the good news of Jesus' birth. Now we can be messengers of this good news: Our Savior is born—Christ the Lord.

Supplies

- Construction paper
- Scissors
- Pencil
- Crayons
- Tape

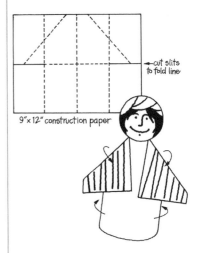

← cut slits to fold line

9″×12″ construction paper

Go, tell it on the mountain, over the hills and everywhere; Go, tell it on the mountain, that Jesus Christ is born.

The Magi Follow a Star

Message:

The magi honored Jesus with gifts.

Greeting with a Gift Bag

Locate representations of the magi in a Nativity set, greeting card, or story illustration. Place the representations in the gift bag.

Greet the children. Hold up the gift bag. Choose a child (or three if you have three magi) to reach into the bag and discover what's inside. Have the child or children show the group.

Ask: Can you guess who these people are?

Say: These are the magi, also known as the wise men. We really don't know how many magi came to honor Jesus. Since three special gifts were given, it's easy to imagine there were three wise men and each brought one gift. The magi followed a star to find Jesus. They honored him with their gifts.

Getting Set for the Story

For each child, draw a star on an index card. The star can be a simple outline or you can color it and/or decorate the rest of the card. Cut the index card into four pieces to create a puzzle. Place each Star Puzzle into a plain gift bag or a paper lunch bag.

Give each child a bag, asking them not to peek inside.

Ask: I brought you a small handmade present. What do you think your gift might be?

Let the children open their bags and bring out the puzzle pieces. Have them put the puzzles together.

Ask: What did your puzzle turn out to be?

Say: I gave you Star Puzzles! Today, we'll hear about the magi, or wise men, who came to honor Jesus. A star is an important part of the story!

Ask children to put their Star Puzzles back into their bags.

Telling the Story

After Jesus was born in Bethlehem, magi in the east saw a bright star. They knew that this star meant that a special child had been born. They wanted to see the special baby, so they got on their camels and went to find him.

The magi followed the star until it stood over the place where the child lived. When they saw the star had stopped, they were filled with joy. The magi entered the house and found the child with his mother, Mary.

Falling to their knees, they honored him. They opened their treasure chests and presented him with gifts of gold, frankincense, and myrrh.

Mary remembered about the angel's message, Joseph's dream, the long journey to Bethlehem, the birth of Jesus, and the visit of the shepherds. She knew that the visit of the magi was one more sign about how special Baby Jesus was.

Exploring

Children will decorate their Star Puzzle bags with foil star stickers. If you don't have star stickers, they can color stars. Purchase small gifts to put inside the bags. Dollar stores are a good place to find inexpensive trinkets.

Invite the children to decorate their bags with stars in honor of the magi, who brought presents to Jesus. Set out the foil star stickers if you have them. Encourage the children to color on any other decorations they want.

While the children work, talk about gifts.

Ask: What is your favorite way to wrap a gift? Do you think the magi's gifts were wrapped? Why do you think we wrap gifts?

Say: I have a surprise for each of you to put in your decorated gift bag!

Place a small gift in each bag.

Say: You may keep your gift or give it to someone as a surprise. When we give gifts at Christmas, we remember the magi who brought gifts to Jesus.

Celebrating with Music

Teach the children "We Three Kings" by playing a recording or singing the song for them.

If you have access to pageant costumes, the children can take turns parading as the magi as everyone sings the carol.

More Exploring

Send the children on a Star Hunt to make Star Cards.

Before Children's Church, place star stickers around a different location at church. Moving to a new spot adds to the excitement and prevents the children from seeing the stickers ahead of time. If another location isn't practical, place the stickers around the room and ask the children not to remove them before the activity. Place about ten stars per child.

Ask: What did the magi follow on their journey to visit Jesus?

Say: In their honor, let's go on a Star Hunt!

Give each child an index card and lead them on the Star Hunt. When a child finds a star, she or he is to remove it and press it onto the index card.

If you have magnetic strips, children can turn their Star Cards into magnets. If not, suggest they use their Star Cards as bookmarks.

Bonus Activity

Study the heavens! Teach the children some facts about comets, look at charts of constellations, or show a craft book that has directions for making beautiful stars. If time permits, consider having the children make one of the star craft ideas.

Saying Goodbye

Give the children their Star Puzzle bags and Star Cards.

Say: We are thankful for the gift from God, the birth of Jesus Christ. We are thankful, too, for Mary, Joseph, the angels, the shepherds, and the magi, who honored the birth of Jesus.

Supplies
- Star Puzzle bags
- Foil star stickers
- Crayons
- Inexpensive gift items

We three kings of Orient are,
Bearing gifts we traverse afar,
Field and fountain, moor and mountain,
Following yonder star.
O star of wonder, star of light,
Star with royal beauty bright,
Westward leading, still proceeding,
Guide us to thy perfect light.

Supplies
- Foil star stickers
- Index cards
- Magnetic strips (optional)

Supplies
- Travel supplies
- Holiday gift bag

Supplies
- Bible

Pray
Holy God, we thank you for sending an angel messenger to Joseph. Joseph obeyed your angel and knew that you were protecting his family from Nazareth to Bethlehem, all the way to the land of Egypt, and all the way back to Nazareth. Amen.

Supplies
- Index cards
- Pen
- Crayons
- Clear tape or duct tape

Travel to Egypt

Message:
God protected Jesus, Mary, and Joseph as they traveled.

Greeting with a Gift Bag
Locate travel supplies such as small containers of shampoo, lotion, or toothpaste, or a travel kit. Place the items in the gift bag.

Greet the children. Hold up the gift bag. Choose one or several children to reach into the bag to discover what's inside. Have them hold up the objects.

Ask: Why would someone need these?

Say: When we travel away from home, we often take personal items with us, things we use every day.

Ask: If you spend a night away from home, what do you pack to take with you?

Say: In our story today, Mary, Joseph, and Jesus had to pack all the belongings they could carry and leave Bethlehem to go to Egypt.

Telling the Story
First, open the Bible and read Matthew 2:13-15 and 2:19-23.

Next review the story by singing the verses of "When the Magi Left" (found on the next page) set to the tune of "London Bridge." For each stanza, sing the first line and the children can then join in. You can sing the last line of each stanza yourself.

Once the children have heard the lyrics and understand the song pattern, they may enjoy singing it again.

Ask: How did God tell Joseph to go to Egypt? How did God tell Joseph to go home to Nazareth? Did Joseph do as he was told?

Say: Joseph took Jesus and Mary to a different country and then back home to Nazareth. Even though these were long journeys, God helped keep Joseph, Mary, and Jesus safe.

Exploring
Children will create a Zig Zag Storybook to review the Holy Family's trips.

Each child will need eight index cards. Before Children's Church, prepare the cards by numbering them 1-8 in an upper corner. You may want to write a caption along the bottom of each card to describe the picture the children will draw.

1. The magi visit Jesus.
2. An angel comes to Joseph in a dream.
3. Joseph, Mary, and Jesus go to Egypt.
4. Here is the family's home in Egypt.
5. Jesus grows from baby to boy.
6. An angel comes to Joseph in a dream again.
7. An angel tells the family to go home to Nazareth.
8. The family returns to Nazareth.

Begin by giving the children the first card. Retell that part of the story. Invite the children to draw the scene. Continue to hand out the cards in numerical order, retell that part of the story, and ask the children to draw the scene. Keep an eye on the time and allow just two minutes or so for each picture. Explain to the children that they may finish the scenes later, after the books are assembled.

Next, have them line up their cards in numerical order.

ASSEMBLING THE ZIG ZAG STORYBOOKS

Plain and Simple: Use ordinary cellophane tape to join the cards at the seams where the card edges meet. You only need to tape one side.

Fancy and Quick: Use duct tape. Fun colors and patterns are available in craft and home supply stores. Turn all the cards drawing-side down. Use one strip of tape to join the cards together from end to end.

Once the cards are taped, show the children how to fold the book back and forth into a zig zag. Have them sign their names on their books.

Celebrating with Music

Teach children the refrain of "God Will Take Care of You." This song is in many hymnals and is available on the internet.

More Exploring

Play the Walk to Egypt Relay Game. Divide the children into two teams. Mark start and finish lines with tape or paper.

To play, line the teams up behind the start line. Give the first child on each team a baby doll. Have them walk quickly to the turnaround, and then walk quickly back to the start. They are to hand over their baby doll to the next person in line, who will then do the same. Play as a relay race or just a fun game.

Bonus Activity

Show the children photographs of ancient Egypt's famous sights, such as the Great Pyramid, the Nile River, and the Valley of the Kings. Your local library will have books on Egypt and/or you can print photographs from the internet.

Saying Goodbye

Give the children their Zig Zag Storybooks.

Say: Today we heard the story of the Holy Family's trip to Egypt and back. May God keep each of you safe until we meet again!

When the magi left, an angel came, angel came, angel came,
When the magi left an angel came, to Joseph in a dream.

Take Jesus and Mary and leave right now, leave right now, leave right now,
Take Jesus and Mary and leave right now
for the land of Egypt.

There they saw the pyramids, pyramids, pyramids
There they saw the pyramids in the land of Egypt.

Then Joseph had another dream, another dream, another dream,
Then Joseph had another dream, to go to Galilee

The family traveled to Galilee, Galilee, Galilee,
The family traveled to Galilee, and lived in Nazareth.

God was with the family, family, family.
God was with the family, just like God's with me!

God will take care of you, through every day, o'er all the way.
God will take care of you.
God will take care of you.

Winter Celebration

Come, let's worship and bow down! Let's kneel before the Lord, our Maker! (Psalm 95:6)

Supplies

- Mitten
- Pocket calendar or calendar page

Supplies

- Dry-erase board or large sheet of paper
- Markers
- Crayons and drawing paper (optional)

The Christian Calendar

Message:
Christians follow the Christian Calendar.

Greeting with a Mitten

Use a real mitten or create one out of paper or cloth. Tuck a pocket-size calendar or a folded calendar page inside the mitten. A calendar page is easily printed from the internet.

Greet the children. Hold up the mitten.

Say: There's something in this mitten that shows the days and the weeks and the month. Can you guess what it is?

Choose a child to reach into the mitten and pull out what's inside. Have the child show the calendar to the group.

Say: We use calendars to help us as the year goes by.

Ask: Can you name some of the months of the year?

Say: Christians use calendars like this one, but we also have another type of calendar. We call it the Christian Calendar.

Telling the Story

Say: Since the beginning of the church, Christians have celebrated the holidays and seasons of our faith. Today, many years later, Christians still celebrate many of the same holidays and seasons. Let's learn more about the Christian Year.

Draw an angel.

Say: The church year begins with Advent. In this season, we get ready for Christmas. Angels told Mary and Joseph the news that they would be the parents of Baby Jesus.

Draw a star.

Say: The next event in the church year is Christmas. At Christmas, we celebrate the birth of Jesus. We see lots of stars at Christmastime on Christmas trees, cards, ornaments, and banners. After Christmas, we celebrate Epiphany. We remember the wise men who followed a star.

Draw the letter J.

Say: The J stands for Jesus. The next season is called the Season after Epiphany. During this season, we especially focus on Jesus' life and the lessons he taught us.

Draw a cross.

Say: The next season is the season of Lent. During Lent, we do many things that will help us grow closer to God. We remember that Jesus died on a cross.

Draw a butterfly.

Say: The Easter season celebrates the resurrection of Jesus from the dead. Jesus came out of the tomb just as a butterfly comes out of a chrysalis.

Draw a crown.

Say: The day of Pentecost is known as the "birthday of the church," and the last season of the Christian year is the Season after Pentecost. The crown symbolizes the Kingdom of God. We are part of God's kingdom, and God loves all of us.

Point to each symbol again and say the name of the corresponding season. Next, lead the children in saying the names of the Christian seasons with you.

If you want to extend the story, give the children paper and crayons and have them draw the symbols as you tell the story one more time.

Exploring

Celebrate the seasons of the Christian year with the following song, sung to the tune of "Here We Go Round the Mulberry Bush." First teach children the lyrics, and then add the motions.

Here we go round the Christian year, Christian year, Christian year,
Here we go round the Christian year at our very own church. *(Roll arms.)*

Advent looks to the coming of Jesus, coming of Jesus, coming of Jesus,
Advent looks to the coming of Jesus, God's gift to the world. *(Point up, then bring finger down to point at floor.)*

Christmas celebrates Jesus' birth, Jesus' birth, Jesus' birth,
Christmas celebrates Jesus' birth, the baby born for us. *(Pretend to rock a baby.)*

Then we learn about his life, about his life, about his life,
Then we learn about his life, Jesus, the Son of God. *(Stretch arms up.)*

Lent helps us be close to God, close to God, close to God,
Lent helps us be close to God because we know God's Son! *(Form cross with arms.)*

At Easter we sing, "He is risen! He is risen! He is risen!"
At Easter we sing, "He is risen! Jesus is alive!" *(Stretch arms out with palms up.)*

After Pentecost, we can sing, "We are God's, we are God's."
After Pentecost, we can sing, "God loves all of us." *(Hug self.)*

Pray

God of Peace, we're glad we can celebrate our Christian faith by following the seasons of the church year. Amen.

Celebrating with Music

Invite a guest musician to play and/or sing some of the songs we sing throughout the Christian year. Encourage the children to sing along.

If this isn't practical, play the songs from a recording or simply lead the children in singing them. Songs can include Christmas carols, Easter hymns, and year-round Christian songs such as "Jesus Loves Me." Don't forget "Happy Birthday" in honor of Pentecost, the birthday of the church.

More Exploring

Children will enjoy Church Year Snacks.

Say: In celebration of the seasons of the Christian year, let's enjoy a snack featuring food from each season.

Cookies: In Advent as we get ready for Christmas, we bake cookies!

Juice: During the Christmas season, we drink holiday punch.

Marshmallows: The Season after Epiphany comes in the winter. In winter, we like to put marshmallows in hot chocolate.

Pretzels: Years ago, many people gave up sugar and eggs and butter for Lent. Since pretzels aren't baked with these ingredients, they were a good food to eat during Lent.

Chocolate: Lots of Easter baskets have chocolate in them, especially chocolate eggs and chocolate bunnies.

Fruit: During the Season after Pentecost, which stretches from late spring to Advent, lots of delicious fruits come into season.

Bonus Activity

Teach children about liturgical colors. Give them slips of paper, lengths of yarn or ribbon, or scraps of fabric or felt in these colors:

Purple: Advent, Lent

White: Christmas, Baptism of Jesus, Easter, Trinity Sunday

Green: Sundays after Epiphany and the Season after Pentecost

Red: Pentecost

(Note: Some churches are now using blue for Advent.)

Have the children hold up a color as you say the seasons and Sundays associated with that color. Then let them take turns holding up a color while everyone calls out what seasons and Sundays that color represents. Let the children take the colors home with them.

Saying Goodbye

Say: Since the beginning of the Christian church, Christians have celebrated the seasons of the church year. We celebrate too!

Supplies

- Cookies
- Juice
- Marshmallows
- Pretzels
- Pieces of chocolate
- Bite-sized fruit
- Small plates and/or napkins
- Cups

Supplies

- Paper, yarn, or fabric in these colors:
  - purple
  - white
  - green
  - red
  - blue (if needed)

Cold Weather Fun

Message:
We enjoy winter, indoors and out.

Greeting with a Mitten
Use a real mitten or create one out of paper or cloth. Tuck several objects related to indoor winter fun inside the mitten. Consider a package of hot chocolate and/or marshmallows or pieces from a board game.

Greet the children. Hold up the mitten.

Say: Inside this mitten are objects that remind us of fun we have indoors in the winter.

Choose a child to reach into the mitten and pull out what's inside. Have the child hold up the objects. Let the children identify them.

Say: There are lots of fun activities in winter, both indoors and out. God created winter, and God wants us to enjoy it!

Getting Set for the Story
Read today's Bible verse, and then ask the children to say it with you.

Say: God made winter! God wants us to enjoy winter activities. Let's see if you can solve some riddles about indoor and outdoor winter fun.

Telling the Story
Are you good at guessing riddles? I bet you are. Here we go!

Outdoors, I stand proud and tall, but if you bring me inside, I'm in trouble. What am I? *A snow man or snow person*

If you hear a pop, you're about to enjoy me for a snack. What am I? *Popcorn*

In the summer you might use me to help you make a sandcastle or plant your garden, but in the winter, people use me to clear their sidewalks. What am I? *A shovel*

I'm shaped a bit like a star, but stars are big. I'm tiny! Stars are hot and I'm very cold. What am I? *A snowflake*

Put one of me on each of your feet, and we'll go zooming down a big hill. What am I? *Skis*

Sometimes horses pull me in the snow, but mostly kids ride on me all by themselves. What am I? *A sled*

I help keep you warm and cozy if you sit near me, but don't touch. I'm hot! What am I? *A fireplace or a wood stove.*

In the summer you can swim in me, but in the winter where it's cold, I'm the perfect spot for ice skating. What am I? *A pond or lake*

I'm red and black, and I march around on little squares. What am I? *Checkers*

When you've been out in the snow, stomp me clean before you come inside or I will make a melty mess. What am I? *Boots*

Bible Verse
You set all the boundaries of the earth in place. Summer and winter? You made them! (Psalm 74:17)

Supplies
- Mitten
- Winter objects

Note
If you live in a climate that has a moderate winter and the children aren't familiar with snow, say a bit about life where the winters are cold. Explain that climates vary all over the earth, and this is part of God's plan for creation.

Pray
God of Peace, we're glad you made winter. We enjoy many activities during wintertime. Thank you, God for winter! Amen.

Supplies
• Paper plates
• Construction paper
• Scissors
• Stapler or tape
• Stickers and/or crayons

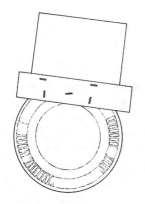

We love winter,
we love winter,
indoors and out,
indoors and out.
Thank you God for winter.
Thank you God for winter.
Indoors and out,
indoors and out.

Read the riddles again. Children will enjoy calling out the answers once they know them. Invite them to make up some winter riddles of their own.

Exploring

Make a sample Snow People Mask to show the children. Fold a paper plate in half. Cut the inner circle from the plate. Unfold the outer part. (You will not need the inner part.)

From construction paper, cut a hat brim about 9 by 2 inches. Next, cut a hat top, about 7 inches square. Staple or tape the brim to the hat and then attach the hat to one edge of the paper plate. Decorate the hat with stickers and/or crayon designs. (Cut paper plates and hat pieces ahead of time.)

Say: In winter, we enjoy lots of outdoor activities. God gave us winter. Even when it's cold, there are lots of things we do enjoy outdoors. In some really cold places people celebrate winter with special winter carnivals. Let's make Snow People Masks to wear in a Snow People Parade!

Assist the children in assembling the masks and decorating the hats. When everyone is finished, have the children line up and march parade-style, calling out, "Happy winter! We're snow people! Happy winter!"

Celebrating with Music

Teach the children "We Love Winter," set to the tune of "Frère Jacques."

Sing other winter songs such as "Jingle Bells" and "Let It Snow."

Exploring Some More

Say: In winter, we like to go outdoors to enjoy winter activities, but we like to be indoors, too, where it's warm. Let's play a game that children played years ago during cold winters. The game is called "Hotter, Colder."

Invite one child to be IT. IT covers his or her eyes or turns in the other direction so he or she cannot see the group. Have another child point to an object somewhere in the room.

IT tries to figure out what the object is by walking around. If IT is moving closer to the object, the children call out, "Hotter!" and if IT is moving away from the object, they call out "Colder!" When IT locates the object, choose another IT and play again.

Bonus Activity

Make old-fashioned cut paper snowflakes using squares or circles of copy paper and scissors. Younger children can fold the paper into quarters and make simple snips to create the pattern. Older children can experiment with more complicated folding and snipping.

Saying Goodbye

Give the children their Snow People Masks.

Say: Winter, summer, spring, or fall, God made the seasons and we love them all! Happy winter! Goodbye, snow people!

Snow! Snow! Snow!

Message:
God gives us beautiful snow.

Greeting with a Mitten
Use a real mitten or create one out of paper or cloth. Tuck a snowflake cut from paper or a drawing or photo of a snowflake inside the glove.

Greet the children. Hold up the mitten.

Ask: There's something very cold inside this glove. What is it?

Choose a child to reach into the mitten and pull out what's inside. Have the child show the snowflake to the group.

Say: In the winter, God gives us beautiful snow.

Ask: Can you each tell me about a time when you played in God's beautiful snow? *(If you live in a climate where it doesn't snow, ask the children to describe a snow activity they would like to try.)*

Say: Listen to a verse in the Bible about snow.

Read the Bible verse.

Say: We're glad that God sends wonderful, beautiful snow!

Getting Set for the Story
Say: For today's story, let's pretend to have some fun in the snow! When I do a motion, you do that motion too. Ready?

Telling the Story
Look out the window! *(Point.)* It's snowing! We've got a snow day. *(Pump arm in air.)* Stand up and get ready to go out in the snow. *(Stand.)*

Let's put on our imaginary coats *(Put arms in coat and then zip.)*, our scarves *(Wrap scarf around neck.)*, our hats *(Pull hat over head.)*, our boots *(Put on one boot, then the other.)*, and finally, our mittens. *(Pull on mittens and clap hands together.)* We're ready! Let's go. *(March in place.)*

Doesn't it feel peaceful out here in the snow? The snowflakes are beautiful. Let's catch some on our tongue. *(Stick out tongue.)* Now let's catch some on our mitten. *(Put palm close to face.)* Amazing!

Let's tromp through the snow. *(March.)* It's so deep!

Let's make a snow ball. *(Pick up snow and pat.)* Let's toss it gently. *(Toss.)*

Brrr! *(Wrap arms across chest and shiver.)* Even though the snow is beautiful, I'm getting cold. Are you getting cold? Let's go inside. *(March in place.)*

It's warmer in here. Let's take off our mittens *(Pull off mittens.)*, our boots *(Pull off boots.)*, our scarves *(Unwrap.)*, our coats *(Unzip coat and pull out arms.)*, and finally, our hats. *(Pull off hats.)* Let's go over to the window and watch the snow keep falling. *(Walk in place.)* I'm glad that God gives us beautiful snow. Thank you, God!

Bible Verse
He says to the snow, "Fall to earth," and to the downpour of rain, "Be a mighty shower." (Job 37:6)

Supplies
- Mitten
- Paper snowflake or picture of a snowflake

Pray
God of Peace, thank you for giving us beautiful snow. Amen.

Supplies

- Copy paper or construction paper
- Crayons
- Stickers or foam shapes (optional)
- Photos of people who will receive the cards (optional)

Snow, snow, snow, snow, snow.
Thank you God for snow!
Snow, snow, snow, snow.
Beautiful, fancy snow!

Exploring

Mitten Cards will send winter cheer to the elderly, ill, or shut-ins in your congregation. Make arrangements to have the cards you make sent to these people. If you have a photo directory, plan on showing photos of the people who will be receiving the cards.

Before Children's Church, fold the paper in half horizontally.

Say: We just took an imaginary Snow Walk, but some people aren't able to go out in the real snow.

Explain who will be receiving your cards and show photos if possible.

Say: Let's cheer these people up by making Mitten Cards.

Have the children hold their hands mitten style (fingers together). Next, demonstrate how they are to trace one hand on the front of the card using the other hand.

Invite the children to decorate their mittens. Encourage them to use bright colors and fun patterns. Offer stickers and foam shapes if you have them.

Have the children color snowflakes around their mittens. They do not have to be white snowflakes. Ask the children to write simple greetings on the inside of the cards such as "Happy Snow!" or "Merry Winter!" Have them write "Love" and sign their names. Admire the finished cards.

Celebrating with Music

Teach the children "Beautiful, Fancy Snow," sung to the tune of "Row, Row, Row Your Boat."

More Exploring

Read some snowy picture books! These books, and other snow stories, should be available at your local library.

The Mitten by Jan Brett. Reproducible pages related to the book can be found at *http://www.janbrett.com*.

The Cat in the Hat Comes Back by Dr. Seuss.

Owl Moon by Jane Yolen.

Snowflake Bentley by Jacqueline Briggs Martin.

The Snowy Day by Ezra Jack Keats.

Snowballs by Lois Ehlert.

Bonus Activity

Lead the children in a round-robin snow story. Begin by saying, "The funniest thing happened the other day when I went out in the snow." Have each child add a line to the story, making it as silly as they can!

Saying Goodbye

Ask the children to pretend for just a minute that each of them is a swirling snowflake as they twirl in a circle waving their arms.

Say: We are thankful that God makes pretty snowflakes! Bye, snowflakes!

Candlemas

Message:
Christians let their lights shine!

Greeting with a Mitten
Use a real mitten or create one out of paper or cloth. Tuck a candle inside the mitten.

Greet the children. Hold up the mitten. Choose a child to reach into the mitten and pull out what's inside. Have the child show the candle to the group.

Say: Today we're going to talk about an old holiday called "Candlemas." On this holiday we remember the visit of Baby Jesus to the Temple with his parents. The candle represents the light of Jesus coming into the world.

Getting Set for the Story
Say: During today's story, every time you hear the word "light," hold your pointer finger high in the air and pretend it's a candle.

Practice this a few times.

After the story is finished, children will each take a turn with a flashlight.

Telling the Story
A good and devout man named Simeon was led by the Spirit to go to the Temple. Meanwhile, Jesus' parents brought him to the Temple according to Jewish customs. When Simeon saw Jesus, he took him in his arms. He praised God and said that Jesus would be a LIGHT to the Gentiles and glory for the Jewish people. Simeon blessed the baby Jesus.

When he grew up, Jesus began his ministry. He set out to explain to people about God. He became the LIGHT that Simeon spoke of. He told the people many important things.

He said, "You are the LIGHT of the world." Then he said that people don't LIGHT a lamp and put it under a basket. Instead, they put the LIGHT on a lampstand and the LIGHT shines on everyone who comes into the house. In the same way, he told the crowd, they should let their LIGHT shine before people, so that others could see the good deeds they do.

As Christians, we are called to let our LIGHTS shine. For centuries, Christians have helped people who are poor, hungry, cold, lonely, sick, and troubled in other ways too. Just as Jesus was the LIGHT of the world, Jesus wants us to shine our LIGHT to help others.

Lead the children in a discussion of ways they let their lights shine by helping other people. Include some of your own actions and those of others in your congregation. Then bring out the flashlight.

Say: Here's another kind of light, a flashlight. It's fun to use flashlights, and it's fun to hear our own names called out!

Explain to the children that each of them will take a turn with the flashlight, turning it on and holding it near her or his face. The rest of the group will say together, "*(Name, name)*, shine your light, show Christian love day and night."

Supplies
- Mitten
- Candle

Supplies
- Flashlight

Pray
God of Peace, thank you for sending Jesus to be a light to the world. Help us to shine our lights as we show Christian love. Amen.

Supplies

- #4 cone coffee filters
- Crayons
- Yellow hard candies
- Tape
- Foil sticker stars (optional)

This little light of mine,
I'm gonna let it shine.
[Hold up index finger and wave it around.]

Hide it under a basket? NO!
[Cover finger with palm. Shout "NO!" and uncover finger.]

Exploring

Make Shine Your Light Baskets to reinforce the concept of Christian service and generosity. Your pastor or visitation committee can deliver the baskets, or you can donate them to an organization that will distribute them.

Children will decorate the baskets by coloring symbols of light such as candles, flashlights, lamps, and the sun, moon, or stars. Foil star stickers add to the fun.

Make a sample Shine Your Light Basket to show the children. Decorate a coffee filter and put five or more hard candies in it. Butterscotch and lemon drops are just the right color, but hard candies in other colors are fine too.

Explain to the children who will be receiving the baskets. Set out supplies. When the baskets have been decorated, have the children write "Love" and their first name or initials somewhere on the basket.

Give out the candies, asking the children to tuck them inside the basket. Tape the baskets closed at the top. Admire the finished baskets.

Celebrating with Music

Teach the children "This Little Light of Mine" by playing a recording or singing the song for them. Once they know the song, show them the motions that go along with it.

More Exploring

Invite a member of your congregation to be a special guest in Children's Church. Choose someone who is happy to discuss how their work (professional or volunteer) shines light into the world. Encourage questions when the speaker is finished and make sure the children say, "Thank you."

Bonus Activity

Groundhog's Day on February 2 is an offshoot of Candlemas, celebrated forty days after Christmas. The weather on Candlemas was said to predict the weather for the next forty days. Check out *www.groundhog.org* for information you can share with the children.

Saying Goodbye

Say: Jesus wants us to let our lights shine. Go into the world and shine your light!

Valentine's Day

Message:
We show love through our actions.

Greeting with a Mitten
Use a real mitten or create one out of paper or cloth. Tuck a paper heart inside the mitten.

Greet the children. Hold up the mitten. Choose a child to reach in and pull out what's inside. Have the child show the heart to the group.

Say: On Valentine's Day, we celebrate the symbol of the heart. We see hearts everywhere!

Ask: When you see a heart, what does it usually mean?

Say: A heart is a symbol of love. One of the ways we can show love is through our actions. Today, as we celebrate Valentine's Day, we'll think about acting with love.

Getting Set for the Story
You will hold up a Happy Heart Puppet to signal the children to respond during the story. To make the puppet, stack two pieces of paper (pink, red, or white). Fold the stacked sheets in half. Cut half of a heart so that when the paper is unfolded, you have two hearts, one on top of the other. Staple the hearts together at the top and sides, allowing room for your hand to slip inside at the bottom.

Draw a happy face on the puppet.

Say: Throughout his ministry, Jesus talked about love, but he also showed his love through actions. He healed the sick, he welcomed children, and he cared about people who were sad and worried. When the Christian church was formed, the early Christians worked hard to carry on Jesus' message of love. Listen to what the Apostle Paul wrote in a letter.

Read the Bible verse, and then have the children repeat it with you.

Say: When we help other people by showing love, our hearts feel happy. Meet my Happy Heart Puppet.

Hold up the puppet. Tell the children that every time you hold up the puppet during the story, they are to shout out "Done in love" in happy voices. Practice this a few times before you begin the story.

Telling the Story
Jessica helps her grandma clear the table after dinner. *(Hold up puppet.)*

Carlos teaches his little brother how to dribble. *(Hold up puppet.)*

Jamal tells his mom every day that he loves her. *(Hold up puppet.)*

Zoey gives her cat fresh water in the mornings. *(Hold up puppet.)*

J. T. introduces himself to new kids who visit his church. *(Hold up puppet.)*

Martine tells her dad that she adores his pancakes. *(Hold up puppet.)*

Asher gives his pastor a high five every Sunday. *(Hold up puppet.)*

Bible Verse
Everything should be done in love. (1 Corinthians 16:14)

Supplies
- Mitten
- Paper heart

Supplies
- Pink, red, or white construction paper
- Scissors
- Markers
- Stapler

Pray
God of Love, we want to show our love through our actions every day. Help us to do all that we do in love. Amen.

Lizzie helps Aubrey learn their spelling words. (*Hold up puppet.*)

Jason and his mom make brownies for a church supper. (*Hold up puppet.*)

Justin collects coins to help feed hungry people. (*Hold up puppet.*)

When the story is finished, ask the children to share examples of their own actions that have been done in love. Add some of your own, too.

Exploring
Children will create Giant Valentines using manila folders.

They can decorate the folders by simply coloring designs on them, or you can offer the optional materials listed. With younger children, it's helpful if you cut paper hearts ahead of time in a variety of colors and sizes.

Give each child a folder. Set out the craft supplies.

Have the children turn the manila folders into beautiful valentines. Encourage them to add words of love. Make sure they sign their names.

When the valentines are finished, have each child show his or her Giant Valentine and say the name of the person he or she plans to give it to.

Celebrating with Music
Teach the children "His Banner over Me Is Love," "Jesus Loves Me," "This Is My Commandment," and/or "Down in My Heart" by playing a recording or singing the songs for them.

More Exploring
Have children make their own Happy Heart Puppets. You may want to cut out the hearts ahead of time.

Set out the supplies.

Help the children staple or tape the puppet pieces together. Invite them to decorate their heart puppets with happy faces. Encourage them to add hair, eyeglasses, jewelry, and any other details they like.

Bonus Activity
Play Valentine Love List! Have the children form a circle. Pass a paper heart, a valentine toy animal, or another symbol of Valentine's Day around the circle. The person holding the object must say the name of someone she or he loves and then pass the object on to the next person.

Saying Goodbye
Give the children their Giant Valentines and Happy Heart Puppets.

Say: Jesus taught us that it's important to love one another. Let everything you do be done in love!

Supplies
- Manila folders
- Crayons
- Paper doilies (optional)
- Colored paper (optional)
- Scissors (optional)
- Glue (optional)
- Valentines and Valentine stickers (optional)

Supplies
- Pink, red, or white construction paper
- Scissors
- Crayons
- Stapler or tape

Lenten Hope

Lent: Growing Closer to God

Message:

During Lent, we do things that help us to know God better.

Greeting with a Lenten Box

Put a few pretzels in the box. Since purple is the liturgical color for Lent, decorate the box with a purple bow or tie it with purple ribbon or yarn.

Greet the children.

Say: We're beginning the season of the Christian year called Lent. During Lent, we use purple in our church. When we see the purple color, we remember that it's Lent.

Choose a child to open the box and take out what's inside. Have the child show the pretzels to the group.

Ask: Yum! What are those?

Say: Years ago, people folded their arms across their chests to pray.

Hold up a pretzel and ask the children to study the shape. Then show them how to fold their arms across their chests with a hand touching each shoulder.

Say: If you look down at your arms, you'll see they are in the shape of a pretzel. Some people say the first pretzel was made during Lent. Lent is the time in the Christian year when we remember that Jesus came to show us how much God loves us. During Lent, we do things that Jesus told us to do in order to grow closer to God.

Read the Bible verse. Invite the children to say the verse with you.

Getting Set for the Story

Say: During the time of Lent, people do things that will teach them more about God and the life of God's son, Jesus. Sometimes they will spend extra time in prayer or in reading the Bible. Often, people will also give something up, like television or chocolate. Years ago, people did not eat rich foods such as butter, eggs, or sugar during Lent.

Tell the children that today's story is a legend. We don't really know if it's true or not, but it helps us think about the significance of Lent.

Come near to God, and he will come near to you. (James 4:8)

Supplies
- Gift box
- Purple bow, yarn, or ribbon
- Pretzels

Explain that the monk in the story's name is Angelo. When the children hear the name Angelo, they are to call out "Go, Angelo!" as they cross their hands over their chests, pretzel-style. Practice this a few times.

Telling the Story

A long time ago, there was a monk in Italy named ANGELO. ANGELO worked in the monastery kitchen baking bread.

One morning, ANGELO began to bake the day's bread. Since it was Lent, he didn't put any butter or eggs or sugar in the dough.

While the bread was in the oven, ANGELO sat down to think and pray. The children in his parish didn't seem to be learning their prayers. He wished he could come up with a clever way to help them. As ANGELO thought, he rolled a leftover piece of dough between his fingers.

In his day, the children were taught to fold their arms across their chests when they prayed. ANGELO kept on thinking as he rolled that piece of leftover dough.

Suddenly, he had an idea! ANGELO twisted the rolled piece of dough into the shape of praying arms.

He put the dough on a pan and baked it. ANGELO got busy cleaning up the kitchen. He left the dough in the oven a bit too long. But when ANGELO tasted it, he decided it was delicious.

"I will call this treat a 'pretiola,' which means 'little reward,'" he said. "My treat will be a reward for the children who learn their prayers."

That very afternoon, ANGELO baked an entire batch of pretiolas. When the children came to the bakery to visit him, he gave pretiolas to those who knew their prayers.

Before long, all the children began to remember their prayers, and they ate batch after batch of pretiolas.

And that's the story of a monk named ANGELO and the very first pretzel.

Exploring

Twist chenille stems into Pretzel Pendants to serve as Lenten reminders.

Make a sample Pretzel Pendant. Cross the chenille stem to create a small circle. Twist a few times at the circle to secure. Next, bend one side and twist around the outside ring. Do the same with the other side.

Cut lengths of yarn or ribbon about 24 inches long, one per pendant. Purple yarn or ribbon is especially fitting for Lent, but any color will do.

Let the children make several Pretzel Pendants, one to keep and the others to share.

Demonstrate how to make a pretzel with the chenille stem. This can be tricky, so encourage the children to be patient as they learn to do it.

Loop the yarn or ribbon through the pretzel and knot the ends.

Pray

God of Love and Hope, Lent is the time in the Christian year when we want to know you better. This Lent, help us to remember that Jesus loved us and showed us how to love you. Amen.

Supplies

- Chenille stems
- Yarn or ribbon
- Scissors

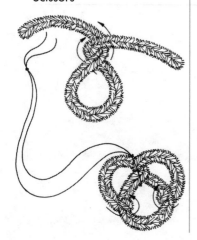

Celebrating with Music

Teach the children the song "Jesus Loves Me" by playing a recording or singing the song for them.

More Exploring

Teach children the story of Jesus in the wilderness, and then lead them in a Wilderness Discussion.

Say: Lent is forty days before Easter, not including Sundays. These forty days honor the forty days that Jesus spent in the wilderness (Matthew 4:1-11). In the wilderness, Jesus was starving because there wasn't any food. The devil came and tempted him by offering him food, but Jesus didn't take it. Jesus proved that he was a servant of God by not giving in to the devil. He was ready to begin his ministry as God's son.

Play the Into the Wilderness Game. One player starts by saying, "I'm going into the wilderness, and I'm taking _____." (The player names something silly or serious.) The next player repeats what the last player said, and adds another item to the list. Play until the list is so long that no one can remember it!

Play more rounds as time permits, specifying categories such as Toys, Games, Supplies, Books, Food, Friends, or Pets that each player takes into the wilderness.

Bonus Activity

Make torn paper crosses out of purple construction paper, copy paper, and/or wrapping paper. Solids and patterns work well together. Cut the paper into smaller sections to make for easier tearing.

Explain that the pieces of torn purple paper should be about as big as a golf ball. Glue the torn pieces onto manila folders or construction paper in the shape of a cross. Explain that a cross is a symbol that tells everyone that we are Christians.

Saying Goodbye

Have the children pick up the Pretzel Pendants they made to share (and their own if they are not wearing these).

Say: Lent is the season of the church year when we learn more about the message that Jesus taught us. During Lent, we think especially about how much God loves us.

Jesus loves me,
this I know.
For the Bible
tells me so.
Little ones
to him belong.
They are weak,
but he is strong.
Yes, Jesus loves me.
Yes, Jesus loves me.
Yes, Jesus loves me.
The Bible tells me so.

Supplies
- Purple paper
- Scissors
- Glue sticks
- Manila folders or white construction paper

Prayer

Message:
When we pray, we grow closer to God.

Greeting with a Lenten Box
Locate a representation of praying hands, such as a necklace, a postcard, or a photograph. Put the representation in the box. Since purple is the liturgical color for Lent, decorate the box with a purple bow or tie it with purple ribbon or yarn.

Greet the children. Bring out the box. Choose a child to open the box and take out what's inside. Have the child show the praying hands to the group.

Say: Tell me about some times when you and your family pray.

Read the Bible verse, and then lead the children in saying it with you.

Say: When we pray to God we are talking to God and saying whatever we feel. But we also remember that God is holy and worthy of our respect.

Getting Set for the Story
As you tell the story, the children will listen for times to pray and respond by moving their arms in big circles out to each side and up, bringing their hands together over their heads and moving them to their chests in an attitude of prayer.

Say: In today's story, the children are finding lots of times when they can pray. Whenever I say, "They decided to pray," I want you to bring your hands to the sides of your legs and then move them way out and up until they meet over your head. Then bring your folded hands to your chest and say, "Let us pray."

Telling the Story
Shondra, Jacob, and Frances ran onto the playground after church. They were glad to be outside. Shondra said to her friends, "I am so happy for this pretty day that I want to tell God 'Thank you.'" So the friends decided to pray. (LET US PRAY.) "God, thank you for this beautiful day." Then they ran to the treehouse.

As they climbed up into the treehouse, they noticed a bird building her nest in the tree. So they decided to pray. (LET US PRAY.) "God, please help this mother bird keep her babies safe."

They enjoyed climbing up the treehouse and sliding down the slide, until suddenly, Frances fell at the bottom of the slide and skinned her knee. As she started to cry, her friends ran to her to see if they could help. They decided to pray. (LET US PRAY.) "God, please help our friend Frances to feel better." Soon Frances had stopped crying and was ready to play again.

Shondra, Jacob and Frances walked beside the flower bed and noticed that the flowers were looking pretty dry. So, they decided to pray. (LET US PRAY.) "God, please send rain to help water the flowers."

About that time, their parents came out to tell them that the church was having lunch together and it was time to come in. As they sat down at the tables with their church family, Pastor Susanna stood up in the front of the Fellowship Hall. And, they decided to pray. (LET US PRAY.) "God, bless this food and the hands that prepared it."

Shondra, Jacob, and Frances were glad they could pray to God at any time.

(Next, ask the children for more examples of times they can pray.)

We don't have to wait for a special time or place to pray. We can talk to God at any time and at any place.

Exploring
Ahead of time, write "I Can Pray for _____" across the top of a piece of paper for each child. Give the children sheets of construction paper and crayons. Ask them to draw a picture of something they would like to pray for. Remember that children are all at different stages of abilities to express themselves. They may choose to scribble with a color that they like. Affirm all drawings.

Celebrating with Music
Sing a prayer song to the tune of "Twinkle, Twinkle, Little Star."

More Exploring
Invite the children to sit in a circle with you.

Say: Let's think about some things we could pray about. Think of people you know who might be sad or sick.

Encourage the children to tell you some people or things they would like to pray for, and write down each thing named. Then, lead the children in a responsive prayer. After you say the phrase below, have the children respond with, "Lord, teach us to pray."

Say: We can pray for _____. (Lord, teach us to pray.)

Repeat until you have named all the things the children listed.

Bonus Activity
If the children are old enough, help them to memorize the version of the Lord's Prayer your church uses by writing each phrase on a separate index card and asking them to put them in order. An easier puzzle to do is to write the Lord's Prayer on a sheet of construction paper and then cut it into several random shapes. Once the children have the puzzles together, help them to read the Lord's Prayer together.

Saying Goodbye
Give the children their Prayer Pictures. Encourage them to hang the picture somewhere where it will remind them to pray to God.

Say: When we pray, we can tell God anything that is in our hearts. God always hears our prayers.

Supplies
- White construction paper
- Crayons

Thank you, God, for loving me.
Thank you for my family.
Thank you for the
winds that blow.
Thank you for the
rain and snow.
Help me learn to follow you.
Be a light in all I do.

Be kind, compassionate, and forgiving to each other, in the same way God forgave you in Christ. (Ephesians 4:32)

Supplies

- Gift box
- Purple bow, yarn, or ribbon
- #4 cone coffee filter
- Crayons
- Scissors
- Yarn
- Stapler

Forgiveness

Message:

Forgiving others helps us grow closer to God.

Greeting with a Lenten Box

Make a Forgiving Face Puppet to put into the box and to be a sample for the upcoming craft project. Decorate one side of a coffee filter with a sad face. Decorate the other side with a smiling face. As well as you can, make the puppet look like you. Consider details such as hair color, skin color, earrings, or glasses. For hair, staple yarn onto the puppet. (If you want to make simpler puppets, use a crayon to color the hair.) Place the Forgiving Face Puppet in the box.

Since purple is the liturgical color for Lent, decorate the box with a purple bow or tie it with purple ribbon or yarn.

Bring out the box. Choose a child to open the box and take out what's inside. Ask the child to hold up the puppet with the unhappy face showing.

Ask: Does this puppet look very happy?

Have the children show you their faces when they are unhappy. Tell the child to turn the puppet around so the happy face is showing.

Ask: Does the puppet look happy now?

Have the children show you their faces when they are happy.

Say: Forgiving Faces are happy faces. Today, we're going to talk about forgiveness. Christians forgive others.

Getting Set for the Story

Children love to hear stories about an adult's childhood. For today's story, come up with one or more examples of forgiveness from your own childhood. Think about how you went about forgiving, even if you have to recreate some of the details. If you have any photos or mementos that can go along with the story, bring them with you.

Telling the Story

God forgives us when we do wrong or hurtful things, and God wants us to forgive others. When someone does something that upsets us, it makes us sad or angry. When we forgive that person, we feel happy. Sometimes, we can forgive someone right away, but other times, it can take us a while.

(Give the example from your own childhood. Next, invite the children to tell their own forgiveness stories.)

When you are angry with someone or your feelings are hurt, that's an extra-good time to ask God to help you forgive. As Christians, we can encourage one another to be forgiving. Listen to what the Apostle Paul wrote in a letter.

(Read the Bible verse. Repeat each phrase and then ask the children to say the phrase with you.)

Paul encouraged the early Christians to be kind, loving, and forgiving to one another. And just as the early Christians worked to be forgiving, we should too. It's not always easy to forgive, but when we do, we make God happy, we make other people happy, and we make ourselves happy too!

Exploring

Locate yarn to represent hair. (For simpler puppets, the children can use crayons to color on the hair.) You may want to precut the yarn in short lengths.

Say: Now you're going to make your own Forgiving Face Puppet to look just like you! On one side, make your angry or hurt face. On the other side, make your happy face of forgiveness.

When the children are finished, put them into groups of two or three. Encourage them to make up small puppet plays in which their characters first get hurt or angry and then forgive one another.

Celebrating with Music

Teach children "This Is My Commandment" by playing a recording or singing the song.

Others songs that work well with the theme of forgiveness are "Peace Like a River," "Down in My Heart," and "His Banner over Me Is Love."

More Exploring

Make I'm Sorry Cards for the children to have on hand at home.

Say: Sometimes, we're the person who needs to say "I'm sorry" and ask others for forgiveness. We can feel shy about saying "I'm sorry." It's good to say it with your voices, but it's nice to have a card to help you. Let's make I'm Sorry Cards!

If you didn't do the writing ahead of time, have the children write "I'm sorry" on index cards. Then ask them to sign their names. Next, invite them to decorate the cards with happy bright designs, and add stickers if you have them.

Say: Your cheerful I'm Sorry Cards are just right to help you say "I'm sorry." Keep them in your rooms. You can bring them out when you want to say "I'm sorry" with a card.

Bonus Activity

Treat the children to Forgiveness Cake! Explain that years ago, when people were upset with one another, they sometimes said they were sorry by sharing a small cake as a sign of forgiveness. Serve snack cakes, inviting the children to use plastic or table knives to cut the cakes into small pieces for sharing.

Saying Goodbye

Give the children their Forgiving Face Puppets and I'm Sorry Cards.

Say: Christians forgive others. What a happy thought and what a happy thing to do!

Supplies
- #4 cone coffee filter
- Crayons
- Scissors
- Yellow, red, brown, and black yarn
- Stapler

This is my commandment, that you love one another, that your joy may be full. This is my commandment, that you love one another, that your joy may be full. That your joy may be full, That your joy may be full. This is my commandment, that you love one another, that your joy may be full.

Supplies
- Index cards
- Markers or crayons
- Stickers (optional)

Note
If children will have trouble writing "I'm sorry," write this on the cards ahead of time.

Supplies
- Snack cakes
- Plastic or table knives
- Napkins

Supplies

- Gift box
- Purple bow, yarn, or ribbon
- Toy turtle or a picture of a turtle

Patience

Message:

Being patient brings us closer to God.

Greeting with a Lenten Box

If you cannot locate a toy turtle or a picture of one in a book or on the Internet, draw a simple turtle yourself. Place the turtle in the box. Since purple is the liturgical color for Lent, decorate the box with a purple bow or tie it with purple ribbon or yarn.

Greet the children. Bring out the box.

Ask: What do you think is in the box? Here's a hint: It moves very slowly.

Choose a child to open the box and take out what's inside. Have the child show the turtle to the group.

Say: It's a turtle! Turtles that live on land move slowly. That's why turtles have become a symbol of patience. Today, we're going to talk about being patient with one another.

Say: When we're patient, we're slow to get angry or upset. God wants us to be patient, especially with other people.

Getting Set for the Story

Ask: Can you each think of a time when you haven't been patient or when a grownup has told you that you're not very patient?

Encourage each child to share an example. Share a few examples yourself.

Say: It's not always easy to be patient when a younger kid is going too slowly on the slide, when grownups won't play with us until their work is done, when our friends are bossy, or when someone who is very old can't hear or understand what we are saying. Love is patient. God wants us to be patient with one another. Listen to a Bible verse about patience.

Read Paul's words in 1 Corinthians 13:4.

Telling the Story

In today's story, some of the kids are doing a good job of showing patience and others are not. Give a thumbs up when someone is showing patience and a thumbs down when someone is not! Ready?

Jalil helped his baby brother get his gloves on the right fingers. *(thumbs up)*

Seth ate the snack in Sunday school before the teacher served everyone. *(thumbs down)*

Rosemary taught her little sister how to tie her shoes, which took about twenty tries. *(thumbs up)*

Jeremy yelled when his dad took too long getting ready to go to the store. *(thumbs down)*

Jason kept his cousins company for hours while their mom was in the hospital. *(thumbs up)*

Annie refused to wait any longer for her sister and went ahead to the playground without her. *(thumbs down)*

Pray

God of Love and Hope, it's not always easy to be patient. Help us to be patient as we live our lives every day. Love is patient. Amen.

Destiny played cards with her grandpa for hours, even though her grandpa didn't seem to remember how to play anymore. *(thumbs up)*

Lee Chin entertained his neighbor's baby by making silly faces and picking up the toys that the baby kept throwing. *(thumbs up)*

Exploring

Turn paper plates into Love Is Patient Turtles! Each turtle is made with two paper plates with paper stuffing in between them. To simplify, the turtles may be made with a single plate.

Write "Love Is Patient" on a plate for each child. You may want to cut out simple heads, feet, and tails ahead of time.

Give each child a plain paper plate and a plate with the writing. Show the children how to staple or tape a head, feet, and a tail onto the rim of the plain paper plate. Ask them to turn the plate over and decorate the turtle's shell with a pattern. Show the children pictures of turtles to let them see the patterns.

Ask the children to put names or initials on the plate with the writing. Then have them turn this plate over so the writing faces down.

Give each child a sheet of tissue, newspaper, or scrap paper. Have them crumple up the paper and put it on top of the plate with the writing. Lay the paper plate with the pattern on top of the crumpled paper. Staple or tape the turtle together.

Celebrating with Music

Teach children "Love Is Patient," set to the tune of "Frère Jacques."

More Exploring

Say: Grownups need to be patient too. Let's pretend we're grownups doing activities that take lots of patience. Ready?

Tightrope walkers go slowly across a tightrope. *(Put arms out to your sides and walk with one foot in front of the other.)*

Trumpeters practice and practice. *(Purse lips and move fingers on a pretend trumpet.)*

Mountain climbers go to the top of tall mountains. *(Pretend to climb.)*

Ministers study and study so they can understand the Bible. Studying helps them learn, so they can teach others about the Christian faith. *(Hold a pretend Bible and move eyes across the page.)*

Writers create books with hundreds of pages. Writing a book can even take years and years. *(Move fingers on a pretend keyboard.)*

Basketball players have to be skilled at dribbling and shooting. Becoming a good basketball player takes lots of practice. *(Pretend to dribble and shoot.)*

Painters create masterpieces. Painting a wonderful painting demands brush stroke after brush stroke. *(Pretend to paint just a small stroke at a time.)*

Say: Good job! You really practiced patience!

If time permits, ask the children what they want to be when they grow up.

Supplies

- Paper plates
- Brown or green construction paper
- Scissors
- Crayons
- Stapler or tape
- Tissue, newspaper, or scrap paper
- Illustrations or photographs of turtles

Love is patient, love is patient,
Yes it is, yes it is,
We will show our patience,
We will show our patience.
Live in love,
Live in love.

Bonus Activity

Teach the children "There Was a Little Turtle."

There was a little turtle. *(Make a fist with one hand.)*

He lived in a box. *(Cover fist with the other hand.)*

He swam in a puddle. *(Make swimming motions.)*

He climbed on the rocks. *(Have the fingers on one hand climb up the other arm.)*

He snapped at a mosquito. *(Clap hands.)*

He snapped at a flea. *(Stick out tongue.)*

He snapped at a minnow. *(Dip hand down to catch a fish.)*

He snapped at me. *(Point to self.)*

He caught the mosquito. *(Grab air with hand.)*

He caught the flea. *(Grab air with hand.)*

He caught the minnow. *(Grab air with hand.)*

But he didn't catch me! *(Point to self and shake head.)*

Saying Goodbye

Give children their Love Is Patient Turtles.

Say: Let your turtles help you remember that love is patient. It's not always easy, even for grownups, but God wants us to be patient!

Loving Others

Message:
Loving others brings us closer to God.

Greeting with a Lenten Box
Before class, create a Möbius strip by making one twist (180-degree rotation) in a strip of paper, then taping the two ends together. Put the Möbius strip in the box.

Since purple is the liturgical color for Lent, decorate the box with a purple bow or tie it with purple ribbon or yarn.

Greet the children. Bring out the box. Choose a child to open the box and take out the Möbius strip.

Ask: See this circle? What do you think will happen if I cut it in half lengthwise with these scissors? Will I have two circles?

Carefully cut the Möbius strip in half lengthwise. The strip will not separate into two strips, but will become one strip that is twice as long and that has two loops in it. Position the loops opposite each other and pinch the strip in the center. Twist one loop around and up to create a heart shape.

Say: Love is like a circle: the more you share, the more there is to share!

Getting Set for the Story
Teach the children the sign language for *love*. Invite the children to cross their hands at their wrists, then press their hands over their hearts. Tell them that when they hear the word "love," they will make the sign.

Telling the Story
Jesus said that we should LOVE one another. One of Jesus' followers, a man named Paul, wrote a letter to one of the churches he had visited. The people in the church had forgotten how to LOVE one another. Paul knew that Jesus wanted everyone in the churches to LOVE one another. So he explained what Christian LOVE is.

He said that even if you knew how to speak every language in the world perfectly, even languages spoken only by angels, if you didn't LOVE, you would just be making noise like a clanging gong or a clashing cymbal.

And if you could understand every book in every library, and had so much faith that you could even move mountains but did not LOVE, you might as well sit down and do nothing.

And even if you gave away everything you had to poor people, and even gave up your life so everyone would think you were good, if you did not LOVE, you could not brag about it.

If you LOVE other people, you are patient and kind. If you LOVE others, you are not jealous, you don't brag, and you aren't arrogant. If you LOVE people, you are not rude, you don't try to get ahead of everyone else, you aren't irritable, and you don't keep a list of everyone who has done something bad to you.

Bible Verse
I give you a new commandment: Love each other. Just as I have loved you, so you also must love each other. (John 13:34)

Supplies
- Gift box
- Purple bow, yarn, or ribbon
- Paper
- Scissors
- Tape

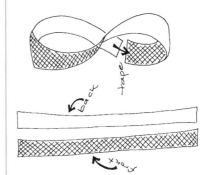

Supplies

- Construction paper
- Markers or crayons
- Stickers or glitter glue
- Hole punch
- Yarn

Jesus taught us how to love,
How to love, how to love.
Jesus taught us how to love,
Love one another.

Supplies

- Cardstock or manila folders
- Scissors
- Permanent marker
- Copy paper
- Crayons (unwrapped)
- Masking tape (optional)

Note

There may be someone in your church who does scrapbooking and may have a paper punch that will make this task easy. Or, you may find cardboard hearts in a craft or teacher supply store.

LOVE is not happy when things are not fair. LOVE is happy only with the truth. People who LOVE put up with all things, trust everyone, hope for everything, and endure everything. In fact, LOVE never ends.

Exploring

Make a Bible Verse Hanging using phrases from 1 Corinthians 13. Take four pieces of construction paper. Write "Love Is" on each of them in large letters. On four other pieces of construction paper, write "Love Is Not." On eight more pieces of construction paper write these words, one word per sheet: "Patient," "Kind," "Trusting," "Happy," "Jealous," "Boastful," "Arrogant," "Rude." If you have more than sixteen children, make two sets of cards.

Distribute the cards and allow the children to decorate them with crayons or markers and stickers or glitter glue.

When the papers are decorated, ask the children to help match up the words that describe what love is and the words that tell what love is not. Place them on a wall or bulletin board, or tie them together by using a hole punch and yarn.

Celebrating with Music

Teach the children "Love One Another" to the tune of "London Bridge."

More Exploring

Ahead of time cut out from cardstock at least one heart for everyone in your class. Write "Love Never Ends" in large letters with a permanent marker on at least one sheet of paper per child.

Have the children place the cardstock heart on a table. If desired, you may tape the heart to the table with a circle of tape on the bottom of the heart. Show them how to place a sheet of paper on top of the heart and rub a crayon over the paper to make a rubbing of the heart. Have them move the paper slightly and make another rubbing with a different color. Continue moving the paper and making new rubbings until the paper is covered with hearts. If time permits, the children may make more than one poster.

Bonus Activity

Read the book *Love You Forever* by Robert Munsch to tell a story about how love does not end no matter what happens. Remind the children that there is nothing they can do that will make God not love them anymore. There are plenty of things they can do that will make God disappointed or sad, but God's love is forever.

Saying Goodbye

Give the children their "Love Never Ends" posters.

Ask them to tell you something that love is and something that love is not.

Welcome Spring!

Message:
God sends us spring!

Greeting with a Lenten Box
Locate one or several items that represent winter (mittens, scarf, ice scraper, mug for hot chocolate) and one or several items that represent spring (gardening trowel, seeds, baseball). Put the items in the box.

Since purple is the liturgical color for Lent, decorate the box with a purple bow or tie it with purple ribbon or yarn.

Greet the children. Bring out the box.

Say: In this box are items that remind us of winter and items that remind us of spring.

Choose a child to open the box, take out the winter items, and show them.

Ask: Why do these remind us of winter?

Next, choose another child to pull out the spring items.

Ask: Why do these remind us of spring?

Say: In old English, the word *lencten* means "spring." Spring comes during Lent. Spring is a wonderful time of year. The weather starts to warm up, flowering bulbs pop from the earth, and new birds appear. Today in Children's Church, we'll celebrate God's gift of spring!

If you live in a place where spring is different from what is described above, you may want to say a few words about spring in your location.

Getting Set for the Story
For today's story, the children will repeat the lovely words from Song of Songs 2:11-13.

Ask: Why are you happy when spring comes?

Say: In Bible times, too, people were happy when spring arrived. They were glad that God sent spring to their land.

Telling the Story
Say: I'm going to read a beautiful passage from the Bible about the coming of spring. I will say a line, and then we'll say it together.

> Here, the winter is past; *(repeat)*
>   the rains have come and gone. *(repeat)*
> Blossoms have appeared in the land; *(repeat)*
>   the season of singing has arrived, *(repeat)*
> And the sound of the turtledove *(repeat)*
>   is heard in our land. *(repeat)*
> The green fruit is on the fig tree, *(repeat)*
>   and the grapevines in bloom are fragrant. *(repeat)*

Say: In honor of the tiny buds and baby birds of spring, let's say the lines as softly as we can.

Lenten Hope

Bible Verse
Blossoms have appeared in the land; the season of singing has arrived, and the sound of the turtledove is heard in our land.
(Song of Songs 2:12)

Supplies
- Gift box
- Purple bow, yarn, or ribbon
- Winter and spring items

Pray

We thank you, God, for sending spring,
for the flowers that bloom and the birds that sing.
Amen.

Supplies

- Paper plates
- Copy paper (white or colored)
- Scissors
- Crayons
- Stapler or tape
- Book with photos or illustrations of birds (optional)

Repeat the verses with soft voices.

Say: Now in honor of the joy we feel when spring is here, let's say the lines in our happiest, loudest voices.

Repeat the verses with exuberance.

Say: In Bible days and nowadays, we're so happy that God sends us spring!

Exploring

Make a sample Paper Plate Spring Bird to show the children. Fold a paper plate in half. This is the bird's body. Color the bird any way you like.

Then fold the plate in half again, so it now looks like a big slice of pie. With scissors, make a one-inch cut about three inches down the folded side. Unfold this fold.

Next, create the bird's wings. If you're using white paper, color the paper if you like. Then fold the sheet of paper back and forth, along the 11-inch length, fan style. Slip the folded paper through the slits in the paper plate. Open the plate slightly and spread out the wings.

To make a beak, cut a triangle out of paper. The triangle's base should be about three inches wide. Fold the triangle in half. Staple or tape the beak inside one end of the bird body with the point of the triangle facing out. You may want to precut beaks for the children.

Say: In many places, birds are a sign of spring! (*Say a word about bird life in your area.*) To celebrate God's gift of spring, we're going to make Paper Plate Spring Birds.

Children may make birds with fanciful designs or more realistic birds. If you have a bird book, let them look at the book for ideas. Have the children put their names or initials inside their birds.

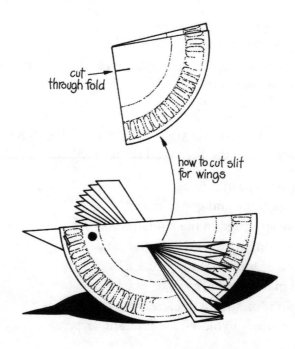

cut through fold

how to cut slit for wings

Celebrating with Music

Teach children "Signs of Spring," set to the tune of "London Bridge," and the actions that go along with each verse.

> Thanks to God for sending spring, *(arms swirling in air)*
>
> Sending spring, sending spring,
>
> Thanks to God for sending spring,
>
> Each and every year!

Here are more verses:

> Thanks to God for cool spring rain . . . *(arms moving up and down, fingers wiggling)*
>
> Thanks to God for birds that fly . . . *(arms flapping)*
>
> Thanks to God for warm spring sun . . . *(arms in a circle over head)*
>
> Thanks to God for bugs and worms . . . *(wiggling fingers pointed at the ground)*
>
> Thanks to God for plants that grow . . . *(arms across chest, then opening wide)*

More Exploring

Play Spring Charades. Write each of the following spring activities on a separate card. You may want to add some of your own.

Supplies
- Index cards
- Marker or pen
- Easter basket, baseball cap, or other spring-themed container

Jumping in a puddle	Opening an umbrella
Digging a garden	Flying a kite
Picking flowers	Throwing a baseball
Swinging a bat	Going on a picnic
Blowing bubbles	Skipping rope
Eating an ice cream cone	Watering a garden

Place the slips in a container that symbolizes spring, such as a baseball cap or an Easter basket. Invite a child to pull out a card and act out the activity while the other children try to guess the correct answer. Let every child have a turn.

Bonus Activity

Make Happy Spring Cards for members of your congregation who are in need of some extra cheer. You can mail these cards or give them to your pastor or visitation committee to deliver. A cone coffee filter, glued onto construction paper, makes a lovely tulip. Children can color the tulip and add a stem as well as other details.

Supplies
- Index cards
- Construction paper
- #4 cone coffee filters
- Crayons
- Glue

Saying Goodbye

Give children their Paper Plate Spring Birds.

Say: Spring is a wonderful time of year. Thanks to God for sending spring!

Bible Verse

Those in front of him and those following were shouting, "Hosanna! Blessings on the one who comes in the name of the Lord! (Mark 11:9)

Supplies

- Gift box
- Purple bow, yarn, or ribbon
- Paper
- Marker

Palm Sunday

Message:

We celebrate the Sunday before Easter with palms.

Greeting with a Lenten Box

Draw an outline of your hand with fingers spread. Fold the picture and put it inside the box. Since purple is the liturgical color for Lent, decorate the box with a purple bow or tie it with purple ribbon.

Greet the children. Choose a child to open the box and take out what's inside. Have the child show the picture to the group.

Say: This is an outline of my hand. In the Holy Land, where Jesus lived, palm trees grow. These trees are named "palm trees" because the branches of the palm tree look like an open hand.

Invite the children to hold up their hands and open their fingers like the branches of the palm.

Say: Palm Sunday, the Sunday before Easter, is named in honor of palm branches. Today, we'll learn why!

Getting Set for the Story

Say: Let's use the palms of our hands to warm up for today's story.

Lead the children in clapping, shaking hands, and giving one another high fives (slapping palms with one another with arms high in the air).

Say: Good job! In today's story, every time you hear the word "hands," hold your palms up high, like this, in honor of the palm tree. *(Hold your hands up in the air with palms facing out and fingers spread apart.)*

Practice this with the children, and then begin the story.

Telling the Story

Jesus and his disciples were coming near Jerusalem. The disciples pointed their HANDS. "Look! We're at the Mount of Olives!"

Then Jesus said to two of them, "Go into the village ahead of you. As soon as you enter, you will find a donkey tied up and a colt with it. Untie them with your HANDS and bring them to me. If anybody says anything to you, tell them the Lord needs it."

He sent them off right away. The two disciples turned and waved a quick goodbye with their HANDS.

When they reached the donkey and the colt, they patted them with their HANDS. Then they used their HANDS to untie them and bring them back to Jesus.

When they returned with the donkey and the colt, they used their HANDS to lay their cloaks over them.

A crowd was in the city to celebrate Passover, an important holiday. The crowd used their HANDS to spread their clothes on the road as Jesus approached. They did this to honor him. Others in the crowd used their HANDS to cut palm branches off the trees, and then they used their HANDS to spread the palm branches on the road.

Pray

God of Love and Hope, we press our palms together as we pray to you today. Thank you for Palm Sunday, a happy day that reminds us that Jesus came to love us and to show us how to live. Amen.

Jesus rode through the crowds. The people in front of him and behind him shouted, "Hosanna, Hosanna!" The people used their HANDS to wave to Jesus. They clapped for joy with their HANDS.

Exploring

Create Pretend Palms in the spirit of Jesus' ride into Jerusalem.

Make a sample Pretend Palm to show the children. Color both sides of two coffee filters green. Next, make cuts from the open end of the filter in to the crimped seam at the bottom. This will create the fronds of the palm. About four or five cuts is best.

Next, cut the filter free at both sides, so that when you open it up, it resembles a butterfly. Press the filter flat. Do the same with the other filter. Put the filters on top of each other. Slip a chenille stem underneath. Bend over about two inches of the stem and twist tightly to secure the filters.

Let each child make one Pretend Palm.

Say: Let's all wave our Pretend Palms and shout, "Hosanna!" in honor of Palm Sunday.

Supplies

- #4 cone coffee filters
- Green crayons
- Scissors
- Chenille stems

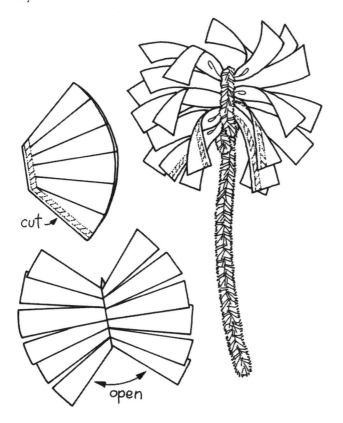

cut

open

Celebrating with Music

Teach children the Palm Sunday hymn "Hosanna, Loud Hosanna" by playing a recording or singing the first verse for them.

Hosanna, loud hosanna, the little children sang;
Through pillared court and temple the lovely anthem rang.
To Jesus, who had blessed them, close folded to his breast,
The children sang their praises, the simplest and the best.

More Exploring

Make Palm Plates for a loved one. Precut yarn or ribbon hangers in about twelve-inch lengths.

Have each children trace one hand onto the center of a plate using the other hand. Younger children may have an easier time tracing one another's hands.

Next, have them write their names across the hands. (It's okay if the name extends past the hand.) Ask them to write today's date at the bottom or along one side of the plate.

Invite the children to decorate the plate any way they like. Punch a hole at the top and tie a yarn or ribbon hanger through the punched hole.

Say: This makes a fancy, fun present for someone who loves you. Every time they look at your hand, they will think of you!

Bonus Activity

Purchase dried dates for the children to taste. Explain that this sweet fruit is the fruit of the palm tree. When dried it was perfect for Bible travelers to carry on their journeys. Sometimes dried dates were even pressed together and made into small cakes. Ask the children if they would like their next birthday cake to be made of dates!

Saying Goodbye

Have the children pick up their Pretend Palms and their Palm Plates.

Say: Remember that Palm Sunday is the day that people spread out palm branches and shouted, "Hosanna!" as Jesus rode into Jerusalem. Palm Sunday is a happy day!

Easter Promise

Easter Sunday

Message:

Jesus is risen!

Greeting with a Symbol

Locate a representation of a butterfly, either an object such as a garden stake or jewelry or a photograph or illustration in a book, magazine, or greeting card. Wrap the representation of the butterfly in tissue paper.

Greet the children. Hold up the tissue paper package. Invite a child to unwrap it and show the butterfly to the group.

Ask: What is this? What do you know about butterflies?

Say: The life cycle of a butterfly begins when the butterfly lays an egg on a leaf or stem. The egg hatches and grows into a caterpillar. When fully grown, the caterpillar attaches itself to a stem. Slowly, the outside skin of the caterpillar hardens into an oblong casing called a "chrysalis." From the outside, it looks like the caterpillar has died. But, inside the chrysalis, the caterpillar is changing into a butterfly. After the change is complete, the butterfly crawls out. Its wings are soft and folded against its sides. In three or four hours, the butterfly unfolds its wings and takes flight.

Ask: Do you ever see butterflies? What do you like about them?

Say: On Easter Sunday, Jesus rose from the dead. When he was buried, his body was wrapped in cloth. On Easter, Jesus came out of the cloth wrappings just like the butterfly emerges from the chrysalis. That's why the butterfly is a symbol of Easter.

Getting Set for the Story

Ask: Have you ever heard of a "tomb," spelled t-o-m-b? What do you think it is?

Say: A rich man named Joseph of Arimathea took the body of Jesus and placed it in a garden tomb. Tombs were either carved into rocks or they were natural caves, so a person who had died was buried above ground in a stone room.

Say: Joseph's tomb was in a family garden. The opening to the tomb was covered with a large stone. Our story takes place in this garden.

Say: You will get into the action of the story by doing different motions. As I read the story about the tomb in Joseph's garden, listen for action clues and watch me!

Telling the Story

On the first day of the week, Mary Magdalene came to Joseph's garden. It was early morning and still dark, but Mary could see that something was wrong with the tomb. *(Put your hand over your heart and look worried.)* The stone had been rolled away from the opening. Mary ran and ran until she came to where the disciples were gathered. *(Tap your feet quickly as if running.)* She told them, "They have taken the Lord away from the tomb, and we don't know where they put him." *(Open both hands wide and place them, palms forward, at either side of your face. Look surprised.)*

Right away, the disciples ran to Jesus' tomb. *(Tap your feet quickly as if running.)* The fastest runner bent down to look inside. *(Bend over at the waist.)* There he saw cloth burial wrappings lying about. Bending over, Peter also looked in the tomb. *(Bend over at the waist.)* He went inside and saw the cloths as well as the face cloth. It was neatly folded away from the other wrappings. *(Open both hands wide and place them, palms forward, at either side of your face. Look surprised.)* The disciples did not yet understand that Jesus had risen from death. They went back to the place where they were staying. *(Place hand over heart and look worried.)*

After the disciples left, Mary stood crying outside the tomb. *(Act as if you are crying.)* Then she bent over to look inside the tomb. *(Bend over at the waist.)* To her surprise, she saw two angels sitting where Jesus' body had been. *(Open both hands wide and place them, palms forward, at either side of your face. Look surprised.)* The angels asked her why she was crying. She replied that the Lord had been taken away, and she didn't know where to find him.

Turning around, she saw a man she thought was the gardener. The man was Jesus. He asked her why she was crying and who she was looking for. Mary told him, and then Jesus said, "Mary." *(Open both hands wide and place them, palms forward, at either side of your face. Look surprised.)* Recognizing Jesus now, she said, "Teacher."

Mary Magdalene hurried to see the disciples. *(Tap your feet quickly as if running.)* She announced that she had seen the Lord. Then she told them all about seeing Jesus in Joseph's garden. *(Open both hands wide and place them, palms forward, at either side of your face. Look surprised.)*

Exploring

Children will create Butterfly Blossoms to remind them of Jesus' new life and the joy of Easter.

For each child, fold a piece of paper lengthwise into thirds. Cut off one third and fold this piece in half in the other direction. Cut a heart from this piece to be a butterfly tail. From the larger piece cut a second heart to be the body.

Give each child a paper plate. Invite them to color a blossom on the plate. Next, give each child a set of wing and tail hearts to color. When the two

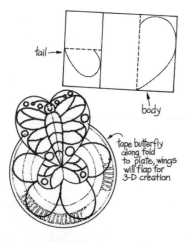

tail →

body

tape butterfly along fold to plate, wings will flap for 3-D creation

Supplies
- Paper plates
- Construction paper
- Crayons
- Scissors
- Tape or glue

hearts are decorated, show the children how to overlap the pointed ends so that the tail point slides under the wing point by about an inch. Tape or glue the hearts together on the back. Finally, use tape or glue to attach the butterfly along the fold to the blossom. This creates a three-dimensional butterfly.

Say: Butterflies have become a happy symbol of Jesus' new life. Let your Butterfly Blossoms express your Easter joy!

Celebrating with Music

Teach children "Christ the Lord Is Risen Today" by playing a recording or singing the first verse of this hymn that Christians all over the world are singing today.

More Exploring

Children will enjoy pantomiming the life cycle of a butterfly.

Say: In pantomime, we don't talk. We use actions to show what we are trying to say. We're going to pantomime the life cycle of a butterfly. First let's practice.

Lead the children in the motions.

Egg Hatching: Tuck head down, place hands over top of head. Then open arms high and raise heads.

Caterpillar Eating: Roll shoulders forward and then tap front teeth together. Repeat.

Inside the Chrysalis: Hold arms stiffly at sides, head tucked, shrug shoulders slightly.

Emerging Butterfly: Hold hands overhead, and then pull arms down to waist level. Repeat three times.

Butterfly Taking Flight: Holding arms down at sides, wiggle fingers. Then raise elbows several times. Next hold arms out at shoulders, and then begin flapping arms.

Say: Now let's do it again. We'll keep silent and really think about each stage of the butterfly's life cycle.

Lead the children in the motions once again.

Bonus Activity

Read the classic children's picture book *The Very Hungry Caterpillar* by Eric Carle and/or show children a nature guide to butterflies.

Saying Goodbye

Give the children their Butterfly Blossoms.

Say: We are Easter People! We believe in Jesus Christ! Alleluia!

Christ the Lord is risen today, Alleluia!
Earth and heaven in chorus say, Alleluia!
Raise your joys and triumphs high, Alleluia!
Sing, ye heavens, and earth reply, Alleluia!

Happy are those who don't see and yet believe.
(John 20:29)

Supplies

- Large plastic Easter egg

Believing in Resurrection

Message:
We believe Jesus rose from the dead.

Greeting with a Symbol
Show the children the large Easter egg.

Ask: What is this? *(Hold up the large Easter egg.)* If you open the egg, what do you see? *(nothing)*

Say: When Jesus died, they put him in a cave—we call it a tomb. Three days later, a woman named Mary Magdalene went to the tomb. When Mary looked inside the tomb, *(Open the Easter egg.)* Jesus was not there!

Say: Jesus was no longer dead. Jesus had risen from the dead. Jesus was alive! But this was awfully hard to believe. Let's hear the Bible story.

Getting Set for the Story
Say: Thomas was a faithful follower and disciple of Jesus. Once when Jesus appeared to the disciples, Thomas was not with them. When Thomas returned, the other disciples told Thomas that they had seen Jesus.

Teach the children the sign for Jesus. Touch the middle finger of the left hand to the palm of the right hand. Then touch the middle finger of the right hand to the palm of the left hand. This sign derives from the story of Thomas wanting to touch the nail prints in Jesus' hands.

Practice this a few times and then begin. Tell the children that whenever you say "Jesus," they should make the sign for Jesus. Whenever you say, "And the disciples said," the children should shout, "We believe!"

Telling the Story
On the same day that Mary Magdalene discovered JESUS' empty tomb, many of the disciples gathered together in an upstairs room. Suddenly, JESUS was there among them, saying, "Peace be with you." He showed them the nail marks in his hands. And the disciples said, "WE BELIEVE!"

Again JESUS said, "Peace be with you," adding, "As God sent me, so I am sending you." JESUS then breathed on the disciples, saying, "Receive the Holy Spirit." And the disciples said, "WE BELIEVE!"

When Thomas returned, the disciples exclaimed, "We have seen JESUS!"

Thomas replied, "I don't believe it! JESUS is dead. Unless I can touch him, I won't believe!" But the disciples said, "WE BELIEVE!"

Eight days later, the disciples were together with Thomas in a house. Even though the doors were locked, JESUS appeared among them. JESUS said, "Peace be with you." He spoke to Thomas, "Look, Thomas. Put your finger here. Look at my hands. No more disbelief. Believe!"

Thomas had no doubts now. He said, "My Lord and my God!" And Thomas and the disciples said, "WE BELIEVE!"

Pray
God of Glory, we're happy believers that Jesus has risen and that he is with us even today. Amen.

Exploring

Children will show their faith by making I Believe Table Tents.

Prepare the Table Tents ahead of time. Use scissors to trim off the folder tabs. If using paper, fold it in half. Pencil "I BELIEVE" in large letters on both sides. Since the I Believe Table Tent will rest on the table like a tent, be sure to orient the lettering so the crease is at the top.

Give each child a folder or folded sheet of paper with the pencil lettering. Have them use crayons or glitter glue to go over the lettering. Invite them to decorate their I Believe Table Tents with the supplies you provided.

Say: Jesus let Thomas see him and touch him, but Jesus told him, "Happy are those who don't see and yet believe." We have not seen Jesus, but we believe Jesus is God's son and that he died on the cross, rose from death, and appeared to his disciples.

Tell the children that the table tents can be used as centerpieces on their dinner tables. Or, they can put them in another location in their home.

Celebrating with Music

Tell the children that you are so happy because you believe Jesus is alive that you want to sing! Teach children "Down in My Heart" by playing a recording or singing the first verse for them.

More Exploring

Use the Belief Bag to demonstrate believing without seeing. Find a few objects that can be identified by touch and put them in a paper bag. Don't let the children see the objects ahead of time. Set the bag on its side on the table with the opening facing away from the children.

Ask: Right now, can you see what's in the bag? Could it be empty? Would you believe me if I told you there is something in the bag?

Say: Come feel the objects inside the bag without looking at them. Don't tell what you feel until everyone has had a turn.

Say: Mary told the disciples that Jesus was alive, but they had a hard time believing until they saw Jesus among them. Thomas said he would not believe unless he could see for himself.

Jesus told him this, "Happy are those who don't see and yet believe." We are those happy people! We did not see Jesus, but we believe.

Bonus Activity

Read the Apostle's Creed to the children. You may want to print copies for the children. Do an image search on the Internet to find artfully designed renditions. Or, use a creed that is used in your church.

Saying Goodbye

Hand out the I Believe Table Tents. Ask the children to hold them high in the air.

Say: Happy are those who don't see and yet believe!

Supplies
- Manila folders or Construction paper
- Crayons
- Scissors
- Pencil
- Glitter glue (optional)

I've got the joy, joy, joy, joy down in my heart. (Where?) Down in my heart. (Where?) Down in my heart. I've got the joy, joy, joy, joy down in my heart. (Where?) Down in my heart to stay.

Supplies
- Paper bag or Gift bag
- Objects to put in the bag

Supplies
- Loaf of unsliced bread
- Tissue paper

Going to Emmaus

Message:
Sometimes we don't understand what we see even when it is right in front of us.

Greeting with a Symbol
Wrap a loaf of bread in tissue paper.

Greet the children. Hold up the tissue paper package. Invite a child to unwrap it and show the bread to the group.

Say: For centuries, bread has been an important part of daily meals. Bread can be made from all kinds of flour from wheat or bean to corn or rice. In the Lord's Prayer, Jesus says, "Give us the bread we need for today."

Say: Jesus was also known to take a loaf of bread and break it into pieces. This is called "the breaking of bread." We'll hear more about this in today's story.

Getting Set for the Story
There are parts of today's story that the children may remember from the three previous lessons. Invite them to count, using their fingers, some of the facts they recognize as the story is told. Or, they may simply raise their hands when they hear a part of the story that they recognize.

Telling the Story
On the same day that Jesus rose from the burial tomb, two of his followers were walking to a village called Emmaus. The men were talking about the things that had happened to Jesus in the last three days. As they walked, Jesus joined them on their journey. They didn't realize who he was.

Jesus asked, "What are you talking about?" The men looked sad. One of them said to Jesus, "Are you the only visitor in Jerusalem who doesn't know what things happened here?" Jesus asked, "What things?"

They answered, "About Jesus of Nazareth. Because of his powerful deeds, he was recognized by God and all the people as a prophet. But our chief priests and leaders handed him over to be sentenced to death, and they crucified him. We had hoped that Jesus was going to save Israel.

"Also, some women from our group went to Jesus' tomb and found it empty. They told us they saw angels who said, 'Jesus is alive.' Some of us then went to the tomb and saw the cloth wrappings. The tomb was empty."

Jesus said to the men, "You foolish people! Your minds keep you from believing all that the prophets said." Then Jesus explained to them everything written about Christ from Moses to the prophets.

When the travelers came to Emmaus, Jesus acted as if he would continue along the road. The two men invited Jesus, whom they still didn't recognize, to stay and have supper. When everyone was at the table, Jesus took the bread, blessed it, and broke it. Then he gave it to the men.

Suddenly, the men understood they were with Jesus! And just as suddenly, Jesus disappeared.

Pray
God of Glory, thank you for Jesus, who loves us and helps us understand things that are hard to understand. Thank you for Jesus! Amen.

Right away, the two men went back to Jerusalem, telling the disciples and other followers that they had seen Jesus and he was really risen from death. Then they told everyone what had happened along the road and how they knew Jesus when he broke the bread.

Exploring

The children will enjoy a bread tasting. (You can use the bread from the Greeting and add a second loaf if need be.) Whipped butter is easiest to spread.

Gather the children around a table. Hand out napkins.

Say: The disciples recognized Jesus when he broke bread. Let's pray.

Pray: Dear God, thank you for this loaf of delicious bread. Bless this bread to the nourishment of our bodies. Amen.

Next, tear pieces of bread for everyone. Give each child a spoon with some whipped butter on it.

Say: Jesus had blessed and broken bread many times with his disciples and followers. In that amazing moment, they understood that this man breaking bread was the risen Jesus.

Celebrating with Music

Teach the children "Let Us Break Bread Together" by playing a recording or singing the song for them.

More Exploring

Ahead of time, cut construction paper in half to make 9" x 6" rectangles. Cut in half again to make 4½" x 6" cards. You will need one of these paper pieces per child. Write "CHANGE HUNGER" on the cards. Make any necessary arrangements for donating money next week.

Invite the children to color pictures of fruits and vegetables, plates of food, or other food designs on the cards. (Optional: Use food-shaped stickers or glue on pictures of food.)

Hand out the storage bags and show how to put the pictures in the bags.

Say: We have blessed and broken bread together today, and our tummies feel happy. However, some people in our community are hungry. Use your Change Hunger Bag to collect coins this week. Bring the bag back here. We'll put the money together and use it to provide food for hungry people.

Bonus Activity

Let the children use play clay to pretend they are making delicious bread.

CLAY RECIPE: In a saucepan, mix two cups flour with one cup salt and three teaspoons cream of tartar. To two cups water, add several drops of food coloring and one tablespoon oil. Stir the water mixture into dry ingredients. Cook over medium heat until the mixture forms a ball. Cool and knead. Store in an airtight container. (Note: The cream of tartar isn't necessary, but helps with elasticity.)

Saying Goodbye

Ask the children to hold up their Change Hunger Bags. Give them each a coin to put in their bag. Remind them to collect coins from others this week and to put some of their own coins in the bag, too.

Supplies
- Loaf of bread
- Butter
- Spoons
- Napkins
- Knife (optional)

Let us break bread together
on our knees.
Let us break bread together
on our knees.
When I fall on my knees, with
my face to the rising sun,
O Lord, have mercy on me.

Supplies
- 1-quart plastic storage bags
- Construction Paper
- Scissors
- Crayons
- Food stickers (optional)
- Magazine pictures of food; glue sticks (optional)

Supplies
- Clay (see recipe at left)
- Table covering

Honor your father and your mother so that your life will be long on the . . . land. (Exodus 20:12)

Supplies

- Flower or representation of a flower
- Tissue paper

Mother's Day

Message:
Honor your mother.

Greeting with a Symbol
Introduce the message by presenting a flower. Use a real or artificial flower, print a drawing or photo from the internet, or locate a photo in a magazine or catalog. Wrap the flower or flower picture in tissue paper.

Greet the children. Hold up the tissue paper package. Invite a child to unwrap it and show the flower to the group.

Say: Today is Mother's Day. Often we give our mothers flowers to tell them how much we love them. Have you done something special for your mother *(or grandmother, or mother-figure)*?

Getting Set for the Story
Ask: Are children sometimes raised and cared for by someone other than a birth mother?

Say: Yes. Some children are cared for by stepmothers. Some children are adopted by a family. Some live in foster homes or orphanages. Other children live with aunts, grandparents, or an older sister or brother. Many children don't live with their first mothers, but they live with someone who loves and cares for them as a mother does.

Say: The Bible tells us to honor our mothers. "To honor" means to treat a person with respect.

Ask: What are some of the ways you show respect to your mother?

Say: In our story, we'll hear how a special mother and grandmother taught a little boy how to love God.

Telling the Story
There once was a boy named Timothy. He was a very lucky little boy, because he had a mother named Eunice and a grandmother named Lois who loved him very much. Eunice and Lois also loved God.

Eunice and Lois heard about Jesus from some of Jesus' disciples. The disciples told the women the good news that Jesus had come from God to tell all the people how much God loved them. They learned the things that Jesus taught his disciples, like "Love one another," "Be kind," and "Love your neighbor as yourself."

Eunice and Lois taught Timothy about God and about Jesus. When Timothy was grown, he traveled with some of Jesus' disciples and told all the people about God's love.

All of the people who heard him were glad that Timothy had a good mother and grandmother who taught him to love God.

Exploring
Fancy Paper Flowers make lovely Mother's Day gifts! Make a sample of each type of flower ahead of time. Decorate both sides of each filter with stripes, polka dots, squiggles, or solid colors.

Pray
God of Glory, we thank you for mothers! Help us to honor them! Amen.

Supplies
- #4 cone coffee filters
- Crayons
- Chenille stems
- Tape
- Stapler

Flower Shape One: Gently turn one filter inside out. It will ruffle a bit, which is good. Next, nest that filter inside a second filter that has not been turned inside out. Lay the top of a chenille stem over the base of the flower and staple or wrap with tape.

Flower Shape Two: Roll a filter into a cone shape, taping the side together. Make two more cone flowers. Join the cone flowers together at their bases by tightly wrapping a length of tape around them. Lay the top of a chenille stem over the base of the flower and staple or wrap with tape.

Hand out the coffee filters along with crayons. Have the children decorate the filters. Next, lead them through the steps for assembling the flowers. Children may make just one of each type of flower or a whole bouquet. Have them put their names or initials on the flowers.

Celebrating with Music
Teach children "Our Mothers," set to the tune of "The Wheels on the Bus."

More Exploring
Play the old favorite "Mother May I?" Line the children up across an imaginary starting line. Stand at a distance from them.

Say: As a fun reminder to honor our mothers, we're going to play a game called "Mother May I?" You'll pretend that I'm the mother. Try to reach me by taking turns asking to take a number of steps toward me. You can ask for Baby Steps, Big Kid Steps, or Giant Parent Steps, but you can only ask for each kind once. You must always ask "Mother may I?" first or you lose your turn.

Call on one child at a time. The children should ask for a certain number of steps each time. You can grant that number or say things like "No, you may not take ten Giant Parent Steps, but you may take five." In this way you can control how quickly the children reach you. If a child forgets to say "Mother May I?" he or she loses that turn.

Say: This is a fun way to remind us that we need to listen to our mothers!

Bonus Activity
Make simple Mother's Day cards using folded paper and crayons. These cards will go nicely with the Fancy Paper Flowers.

Saying Goodbye
Give children their Fancy Paper Flowers.

Say: The Bible tells us to honor our mother and father. Even on the cross, Jesus showed his love and respect for his mother, Mary. Let's thank the mother who cares for us and honor her on Mother's Day and every day!

At home our mothers smile and hug,
Smile and hug, smile and hug.
At home our mothers smile and hug,
Showing love this way!

At home our mothers teach us things…

At home our mothers care for us…

At home our mothers help us pray…

Supplies
- Construction paper
- Crayons

As they were watching, [Jesus] was lifted up and a cloud took him out of their sight. (Acts 1:9)

Supplies

- Cotton balls (stretched so that they cling to one another) or sheet of rolled first-aid cotton
- Construction paper or cardboard
- Tissue paper

Pray

God of Glory, you brought your Son Jesus to heaven in a cloud of glory. We thank you for sending Jesus to lead us and teach us. Amen.

Supplies

- Cotton balls
- Large unlined index cards
- Marker
- Glue
- Magnetic stripping (optional)

Jesus Ascends into Heaven

Message:

Jesus goes to heaven to be with God.

Greeting with a Symbol

Press cotton balls into a cloud shape and then place the cotton ball cloud on a base of construction paper or cardboard. (There is no need to glue down the cotton ball cloud.) Wrap the cloud in tissue paper.

Greet the children. Hold up the tissue paper package and then unwrap it.

Say: This is a pretend cloud. A cloud is a symbol of the moment Jesus left the earth and went up to heaven to be with God.

Getting Set for the Story

Say: Our story is about when Jesus rose to heaven. We call this the Ascension of Jesus. To *ascend* means to go up. As you listen to the story, you can hold a piece of our cloud in your hand.

Telling the Story

After Jesus rose on Easter, he stayed with the disciples to continue to teach them all they would need to know. He stayed with them over a period of forty days, speaking to them about God's kingdom.

However, at the end of the forty days, he told them it was time for him to return to heaven to be with God. Before he went, he told the apostles to go into the world and teach all the people about God's love. And even though they would no longer see his body with them, he would always be with them, in their hearts.

After Jesus said these things, and while the apostles were watching him, he was lifted up and a cloud took him out of their sight. As Jesus was going away, the apostles were staring up toward heaven. Suddenly, two men in white robes stood next to them. They said, "Don't just stand here looking up into heaven. Go and do what Jesus told you to do." So the apostles returned to Jerusalem to get ready to tell the world about Jesus and about God's love.

Exploring

Honor the Ascension by making Scripture Clouds. Use the cotton balls from the Greeting, adding more if needed.

Prepare an index card for each child by printing "Acts 1:9" along the edge. You may want to write part of the verse, too: "A cloud took him out of their sight."

Make a sample Scripture Cloud to show the children. Glue a single layer of cotton balls to the card. Tacky craft glue, which dries quickly, can be used if you want the cards to have more than a single layer of cotton balls.

Ask: In our story, when Jesus finished talking with his apostles, what amazing thing happened to him? Where was Jesus going on the cloud?

Say: Ascension Sunday is the Sunday we honor Jesus ascending into heaven, going up to God.

Hold up the sample Scripture Cloud.

Say: Use your imagination and some cotton balls to create a Scripture Cloud to honor the Ascension of Jesus.

Give each child a card. If you have magnetic stripping, have the children attach this to the back of their card. With the magnetic stripping, the cards will stick to a refrigerator, file cabinet, or other metal furniture.

Invite children to create fluffy clouds. When everyone is finished, admire the clouds and set them aside.

Celebrating with Music
Teach children "Hallelu, Hallelujah" by playing a recording or singing the song for them.

If the children know this song, divide the group in half. Have group one sing "Hallelujah" and group two sing "Praise Ye the Lord."

More Exploring
Play a game of Musical Clouds. Give each child a sheet of white paper. Invite them to cut a cloud from the paper (or make the clouds ahead of time).

When the clouds are cut, have the children stand in a wide circle. Ask them to place their clouds on the floor and then put a foot on top of them.

Explain the game: As you play music, the children will move around the circle to the rhythm of the song. You will reach in to remove one cloud, and then stop the music. The child without a cloud to stand on will stand aside. Then you will hand the cloud to the child and say, "*(Child's name)* is in the clouds." The child will step aside. As more children are called out, have them stand with this child.

Repeat the steps of the game until only one child remains.

Say: Everyone is in the clouds!

Bonus Activity
Make Tasty Cloud Treats by squirting pressurized whipped cream or scooping marshmallow cream onto graham crackers. Tell the children they are enjoying a heavenly snack!

Saying Goodbye
Hand out the Scripture Clouds. Children may take a paper cloud, too, if they choose.

Lead them in reciting today's Bible verse.

Say: The cloud is a symbol of the Ascension, when Jesus went to heaven to be with God. We thank God for Jesus' time on this Earth and for Jesus' place forever in heaven.

Hallelu, Hallelu, Hallelu, Hallelujah!
Praise ye the Lord!
Hallelu, Hallelu, Hallelu, Hallelujah!
Praise ye the Lord!
Praise ye the Lord, Hallelujah,
Praise ye the Lord, Hallelujah,
Praise ye the Lord, Hallelujah,
Praise ye the Lord!

Supplies
- Large sheets of white paper
- Scissors
- Music player
- Recording of appropriate music

Note
Be very sensitive if a child interprets the game as saying that they have died. Assure them that this is only a game.

Supplies
- Whipped cream or Marshmallow cream
- Graham crackers
- Napkins

When Pentecost Day arrived, they were all together in one place. (Acts 2:1)

Supplies

- Yellow, orange, or red paper
- Scissors
- Tissue paper

Pentecost

Message:

The Holy Spirit helped the apostles tell the world about Jesus.

Greeting with a Symbol

Cut a flame shape from colored paper. Wrap the flame in tissue paper.

Greet the children. Hold up the tissue paper package. Invite a child to unwrap it and show the flame to the group and ask them to guess what it is.

Say: When a fire burns, it's made up of separate flames that leap and flicker.

In our story today, the Holy Spirit comes to the apostles with flames that flicker over the heads of each one. That's why a flame is a symbol of the time the Holy Spirit came to the apostles. That day is called "Pentecost." The church celebrates Pentecost because on this day, the Holy Spirit helped the apostles tell the world about Jesus in special and holy ways.

Getting Set for the Story

You will lead the children in hand motions during the story. Practice the motions together before you begin.

Say: Now we'll use these motions as we hear today's Bible story.

Telling the Story

On the day of Pentecost, when all the apostles were together, a sudden sound like the howling of a fierce wind filled the whole house! *(Cup both hands around mouth and say, "Woo-woo.")*

Then they saw what seemed to be flames over one another's heads. *(Put hands above head and wiggle fingers.)* The Holy Spirit filled them, and they were able to speak in different languages. *(Cup hand around ear.)*

Outside the house, when they heard howling winds, a crowd gathered. *(Shade eyes and look from side to side.)* The people in the crowd were from many countries and spoke many languages, but everyone heard the apostles speaking in a language they could understand.

The crowd was surprised, saying, "How can these men from Galilee speak in these languages? What does it mean?"

The Apostle Peter stood and got the attention of the crowd. He called out *(Cup hands over mouth.)*, "God proved that Jesus of Nazareth was the Christ through miracles, signs, and wonders. Jesus was crucified *(Make cross with fingers.)*, but God raised him from death *(Point to heaven.)* and gave Jesus the power of the Holy Spirit. Jesus has poured out the Holy Spirit on the apostles. What you see and hear comes from him."

When the crowd heard this, they were troubled. *(Place hand over mouth.)* They asked, "What can we do?" Peter said, "Change your hearts and your lives. Believe that Jesus is the Son of God."

Those who accepted Peter's message were baptized. *(Touch fingers to forehead.)* God brought about three thousand believers to the community of Christ that day. *(Clap hands.)*

Pray

God of Glory, thank you for the gift of the Holy Spirit, sent to the apostles by Jesus. We, too, believe the Holy Spirit can be our helper. Amen.

Exploring

Make a sample Holy Spirit Wind Spiral to show the children. On the bottom of a paper plate, use a pencil to mark about an inch and a half–wide spiral from the outer edge of the plate to the center.

Turn the plate over. Use crayons to color the plate with red, yellow, and orange in any pattern you like. Turn the plate back over and follow the guidelines to cut the spiral. Add a twelve-inch yarn or ribbon hanger to the center of the spiral by tying it through a punched hole or by stapling.

Mark the pencil lines on the plates for the children ahead of time. It's helpful to cut the yarn or ribbon hangers, too.

Say: The Holy Spirit came at Pentecost with the sound of howling wind. Flames appeared over the heads of the disciples. To remember the wind, we're going to make Holy Spirit Wind Spirals. To remember the flames, we'll color the wind spirals red and orange and yellow.

After the children color their plates, have them follow the penciled lines to cut the spirals. Next, attach the lengths of yarn or ribbon.

Celebrating with Music

Teach children "Spirit of the Living God" by playing a recording or singing the song for them.

More Exploring

Sing and sway with a Christian Sing-a-Long! Plan to play songs such as "Every Time I Feel the Spirit," "This Little Light of Mine," "Rise and Shine," and other standards. Give each child a streamer.

Say: Let's feel the Spirit as we sing, sway, and wave our streamers to express the joy of the music!

Bonus Activity

Pentecost is considered the birthday of the church! Bring in a cake or cupcakes. Sing "Happy Birthday" and celebrate two thousand years of Christianity.

Saying Goodbye

Give the children their Holy Spirit Wind Spirals. If you used streamers, gives these to the children, too.

Say: Jesus promised to send the Holy Spirit to be our companion and helper. The Holy Spirit didn't just come for the apostles, but came for all Christian believers, including you and me!

Supplies
- Paper plates
- Pencils
- Scissors
- Crayons
- Yarn or ribbon
- Hole punch or stapler

Supplies
- Crepe paper streamers, ribbon, or fabric strips
- Recorded music of Bible songs
- Music player

Supplies
- Birthday cake or cupcakes
- Napkins
- Paper plates

Bible Verse
We can be encouraged by the faithfulness we find in each other. (Romans 1:12)

Supplies
- Bible
- Tissue paper

Supplies
- #4 cone coffee filters
- Crayons

Pray
God of Glory, we are glad for the time we can be together to talk about Bible stories. We encourage one another to have a strong faith in your son, Jesus. Amen.

Encouraging the Faith

Message:
We help each other have a strong faith in Jesus.

Greeting with a Symbol
Wrap the Bible in tissue paper.

Greet the children. Hold up the tissue paper package. Invite a child to unwrap the Bible and show it to the group.

Say: This is our holy book, the Bible. From the Bible we learn stories, lessons, laws, wise sayings, and prayers that guide us as Christians. As Christians, we help one another have a strong faith in Jesus.

Getting Set for the Story
Give each child two coffee filters. Ask them to draw their own face on one filter and the face of a friend on another. Have the children put names on both puppets.

When the puppets are finished, have the children place their "You" Handy Puppet on one hand and their "Friend" Handy Puppet on the other.

Invite the children, one at a time, to introduce their puppets, first saying their own name and then their friend's name.

Explain that the puppets will take turns speaking during the story. When the children hear "You say," they will repeat the line using the You Handy Puppets. When they hear "Your friend," they will repeat the line using the Friend Handy Puppets.

Telling the Story
As Ms. Grace played the last piano key, Ms. Lee praised the Joyful Noise Choir and invited the children to join their leaders for Sunday school.

In the Pre-Kindergarten class, the leader read the story of Jesus blessing the children. You say, "Parents brought their kids to see Jesus." *(repeat)* Your friend says, "Jesus placed his hands on them and prayed." *(repeat)* You say, "Jesus said the kingdom of heaven is for people like us." *(repeat)* Your friend says, "Jesus loves us." *(repeat)*

In the Kindergarten–First Grade class, the leader told the story of the Feeding of the Five Thousand. You say, "Jesus was preaching to five thousand people!" *(repeat)* Your friend says, "And all those people got hungry!" *(repeat)* You say, "A boy offered five loaves of bread and two fish." *(repeat)* Your friend says, "And the people ate as much as they wanted!" *(repeat)*

In the Elementary Group, the leader shared the story of Jesus visiting the Jerusalem Temple when he was twelve years old. You say, "After Passover, Jesus' family and friends were traveling home." *(repeat)* Your friend says, "At the end of the day, Jesus' parents couldn't find him." *(repeat)* You say, "They hurried back to Jerusalem to find Jesus." *(repeat)* Your friend says, "Three days later, his parents found him in the Temple." *(repeat)*

Exploring

Continue using the Handy Puppets to engage in the following discussion.

Ask the questions in a relaxed manner, calling upon volunteers first, and then encouraging quieter children to make a comment. If a good discussion develops, there is no need to complete the questions. Children will have their You Handy Puppets answer the questions:

- What is your favorite Bible story?
- Do you have a favorite Bible song? *(Sing the songs if time permits.)*
- Do you have a favorite Bible verse?
- Can you remember a favorite mealtime prayer? Bedtime prayer?
- Is there a favorite person or place that helps you enjoy your faith?

Thank the Handy Puppets for their participation. Set the puppets aside.

Celebrating with Music

Teach children the song "His Banner over Me Is Love" by playing a recording or singing the song for them.

Next, show them these actions: The Lord (point heavenward); I (point to self); Banner (raise arms from sides to touch with fingertips over head); Love (place hand over heart).

More Exploring

Encourage one another as Faith Flag Cheerleaders!

Ahead of time, assemble a Faith Flag for each child and one for yourself. Cut sheets of construction paper in half diagonally. On each paper flag, print "1 Cor. 13:4-7." Using tape, secure the straw to the wide end of the flag.

Present a flag to each child. Invite the children to decorate their flags.

Say: Today, let's use Faith Flags to be Christian cheerleaders! Cheerleaders encourage the crowd to cheer and this helps the team feel good and strong. As Christian cheerleaders, we want to encourage others to feel good and strong about their faith in Jesus.

Say: On our Faith Flag is a Bible verse clue. It stands for First Corinthians, Chapter 13, verses 4-7. We'll use this verse to cheer about love.

Read the verses one phrase at a time and encourage the children to shout each phrase back to you.

You are cheerful cheerleaders! Well done! *(Clap.)*

Bonus Activity

Invite one or more teenagers in your congregation to visit Children's Church to describe their experiences in youth group, Sunday school, and other activities. Encourage the children to ask questions.

Saying Goodbye

Give children their Handy Puppets and Faith Flags.

Say: This week, practice talking to your friends and family about Jesus so you can help one another have a strong faith. Goodbye, Cheerleaders!

The Lord is mine and I am his,
His banner over me is love.
[repeat twice]
His banner over me is love.

Supplies

- Construction paper
- Plastic drinking straws
- Scissors
- Tape
- Marker
- Crayons
- Bible

God's Garden

Bible Verse

Other seed fell on good soil and bore fruit.
(Matthew 13:8)

Supplies

- Garden pot
- Packet of easily grown flower seeds (such as zinnia or marigold)
- Packet of vegetable seeds that are a larger size (such as beans or squash)

Seedtime

Message:
God created seeds and soil.

Greeting with a Garden Pot
Place a packet of flower seeds and a packet of vegetable seeds into a garden pot.

Greet the children. Hold up the garden pot.

Ask: How do we use this kind of container?

Say: You're right! We grow plants in garden pots. There are flowers, vegetables, and herbs that grow well in garden pots. This is sometimes called "container gardening." Now let's see what is inside this pot!

Choose a child to reach in the pot to reveal the seed packs. Invite the child or the group to name the surprise.

Say: God created seeds and the soil seeds grow in. Today we're going to see and learn about God's seeds and how to plant them in soil.

Telling the Story
Emma and Forest wanted to plant a garden. Grandma took the kids to a garden store to buy the things they needed for a container garden. She pulled out a shopping cart and led the way to the racks of seeds.

Emma and Forest looked at the beautiful pictures of vegetables, flowers, and herbs on the seed packs.

Emma pulled out a pack showing a pile of small, bright orange pumpkins. Forest found a pack of green bean seeds. "I like to eat green beans," he said.

Grandma held up a pack of lettuce seeds. She said, "Lettuce grows pretty quickly. Let's grow our own salad!"

Then Emma spotted a pack of brightly colored flower seeds. "What are these, Grandma?"

"They're zinnias and they're easy to grow. They will give you lots of flowers for inside and outside. Now, children, choose one more seed pack each."

"I want to grow watermelons!" Forest said.

Emma laughed. "Forest, every plant you grow will be green!"

Emma reached for a pack of red cherry tomato seeds, adding, "Everything I'll grow will have bright colors."

"Together it will make a wonderful garden," said Grandma as she put bags of potting soil in the cart.

Once they were home, the kids decided where to place their new garden pots. Then Grandma helped them fill the pots with soil from the store. Grandma explained they should water the soil before planting the seeds because the soil was dry.

Finally, it was time to plant the seeds. One by one, Grandma read the directions from each of the six seed packs. Emma and Forest planted seeds for pumpkins, green beans, lettuce, zinnias, baby watermelons, and cherry tomatoes. Very gently, they watered the seeds that sat just below the top soil.

Everyone stood back to admire the container garden. "Just imagine how pretty it will be," said Emma.

"And how yummy it will taste!" Forest replied.

Exploring

Invite the children to examine seeds and then make Seedtime Markers.

Before Children's Church, cut index cards in half. Each child will use one half of an index card for each marker.

Begin by opening the seed packs and pouring each kind of seed on a different plate. Have the group look at the seeds on each plate and then the packet pictures of the fully-grown plants.

Ask: Do the seeds look anything like the fully-grown plants in the pictures?

Say: They truly do look different. The Bible says, "What you put in the ground doesn't have the shape that it will have. . . . God gives it the sort of shape that he chooses, and he gives each of the seeds its own shape" (1 Corinthians 15:37-38).

Ask: As you look at the plates of seeds, do you see different shapes?

Say: God created seeds and each has its own shape. When a plant is grown and the vegetable or flower is ready to be picked, that's when the seeds inside the plant are also fully grown and ready to plant.

Next, have the children decide which seeds they would like to grow, but do not let them take any seeds yet.

Say: When we plant seeds in the soil, we might forget what kind of seeds they are or where we put them. That's why it's a good idea to use garden markers. You're going to make your own Seedtime Markers for the seeds you've chosen.

Hand out the index card halves and crayons. Ask the children to decorate their markers to look like the seed or the plant and/or to write the name of the plant on the marker.

When the Seedtime Markers are finished, have the children put their names or initials on the back. Finish by taping each card to a drinking straw or a craft stick. Set them aside.

Pray
God of Seedtime and Harvest, we thank you for all types of seeds and their interesting shapes. Thank you for the amazing seeds you created for us! Amen.

Supplies
- Seed packets from Greeting
- Index cards
- Scissors
- Paper plates
- Crayons
- Drinking straws or craft sticks
- Tape

We will choose a little seed, little seed, little seed.
We will choose a little seed and put it in the soil.

Soon we'll see it sprout and grow, sprout and grow, sprout and grow.
Soon we'll see it sprout and grow into a pretty plant.

Supplies

- Peat cups or paper cups
- Potting soil
- Spoons
- Seeds on plates and Seedtime markers from Exploring
- Ruler
- Plastic sandwich bags

Supplies

- Popped corn, shelled and roasted sunflower seeds, or roasted pumpkin seeds
- Napkins
- Cups
- Water or juice

Celebrating with Music
Teach children "The Little Seed," set to the tune of "Mary Had a Little Lamb."

More Exploring
Plant seeds in Seedtime Cups to share the wonder of seeing a plant grow!

If you have a large group, you will need a helper or two. Pour the potting soil into another container to make the project less messy.

Say: In the Bible, God said, "Let the earth grow plant life: plants yielding seeds and fruit trees bearing fruit with seeds inside it, each according to its kind throughout the earth" (Genesis 1:11). God created seeds, and God is glad when we put seeds in soil. We can see how those seeds grow!

Assist each child in scooping soil into the cups, about two-thirds full.

Focusing on one type of seed, give the children the prepared Seedtime Markers and set out the matching seed plate.

Read the seed pack directions regarding the depth for planting each type of seed. Use the ruler to push an indentation in the soil to the proper depth. Give children the seeds and tell them to put the seeds in the spot you made. Sprinkle a bit of soil to cover the indentation in each cup.

Have each child put the correct marker in the cup. Place the cup in a sandwich bag and seal the bag, so that the dirt and seed stay within the bag until they get home. Assure the child that if the seed comes out of the dirt (if the pot spills while being transported), it can be replanted when the child gets home.

Repeat these steps with the remaining seed types.

Say: Gently water your seeds once a day with a tablespoon or two of water. Do not let the dirt get soggy. Put the cup in or near a window. Watch for the seeds to sprout. When the plant has six healthy leaves on it, the plant may be carefully moved from the Seedtime Cup to a bigger pot or into the ground.

Bonus Activity
Serve a seed snack! Popped corn, shelled and roasted sunflower seeds, and roasted pumpkin seeds are fun treats to try. Serve with water or juice.

Saying Goodbye
Give children their Seedtime Cups.

Say: Be a happy part of God's garden by taking care of your plants!

Plants Need Sunshine

Message:
God created the sun and the earth.

Greeting with a Garden Pot
Draw a simple picture of the sun. Put the picture in the pot.

Greet the children. Hold up the garden pot.

Ask: If you could plant any seed you wanted in this pot, what would you choose?

Say: What a fun garden those seeds would make! Now let's look in the garden pot to see what's inside.

Choose a child to reach in the pot to reveal the sun picture. Invite the child or the group to name the surprise.

Say: There are many kinds of seeds in the world and most of them need light to sprout and grow. Plants, people, and other creatures on earth need the sun! God created the sun and the earth. The sun is an important part of life.

Getting Set for the Story
The characters in the story are plants in a garden. Daisy and Tater ask the questions about the sun. Sage and Butternut provide the answers.

When the children hear Daisy's name, they will spread open the fingers of both hands, like flower petals. When they hear Tater's name (slang for potato), they will make fists and wiggle their wrists.

Practice the actions that go with each name and then begin.

Telling the Story
The dawn began to lighten the night sky. In the garden, DAISY asked, "What is happening?"

Sage answered, "This is called *dawn*. It's a short time just before the sunrise when the sky gets brighter."

DAISY, TATER, Sage, and Butternut quietly watched the soft yellow and rosy pink colors appear in the eastern sky.

TATER broke the silence with a question. "So what's the sunrise?"

Butternut said, "It's when we can see the big bright circle of the sun rising up from the land."

TATER asked, "Is that the sun peeking over the hill?"

"Yes," said Sage.

The birds began to chirp and sing. The plants in the garden stretched up toward the sun. Butternut's big yellow flowers opened. In a while, DAISY said, "My roots are warming up. Why is that happening?"

Butternut answered, "The sun warms everything it shines on. The soil warms up when the sun shines on it."

Supplies
- Paper plates
- Yellow, orange, and pink construction paper
- Glue
- Scissors (optional)

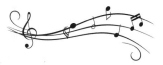

Jesus, Jesus,
Jesus in the morning,
Jesus at the noontime.
Jesus, Jesus
Jesus when the sun goes down.

Love him …

Serve him …

Supplies
- Manila folders
- Wide tape
- Scissors
- Crayons

The day passed slowly. The plants turned their stems just a bit to follow the sun as it moved across the sky.

Sage said, "Look to the west. The sun is setting."

DAISY asked, "Does this mean the day is over?"

Sage said, "Yes, it will soon become dark. The air and the soil will cool down. It's a good time to rest."

TATER said, "I see a star. I'm ready to say goodnight."

"See you in the morning," said Sage.

Exploring
Tear or cut the paper into irregular pieces from golf ball–size to tennis ball–size.

Give everyone a plate. Have the children glue the paper sun pieces onto their plates. Demonstrate how the pieces can be overlapped. The pieces can also extend over the edge of the plate to create sun rays. As the children work, admire their beautiful suns and make sure they are gluing the pieces down securely. Have them write their names or initials on the back of their plates.

Next, have everyone stand, holding their Sunshine Plates in their right hands, with their left hands at their sides. Lead the group in saying "Sunrise" with arm and Sunshine Plate straight out from shoulder, "High noon" with hand and plate above head, and "Sunset" with arm crossed in front of the body to the left shoulder. Repeat, inviting the children to take turns leading.

Celebrating with Music
Teach the children "Jesus in The Morning" by playing a recording or singing the song to the children. Use the Sunshine Plates as they sing.

More Exploring
If it is Father's Day, make a Messenger Bag as a gift for dads.

Locate two-inch–wide tape. Bright-colored tapes can be found in hardware stores or hardware departments and patterned decorative tapes can be found in craft stores or craft departments. If you can't find fancy tape, packing tape will work.

Prepare manila folders by trimming off the tabs. Next, secure each nine-inch side with a nine-inch strip of tape. On one side, attach one inch of the two-inch width. Turn the folder over and press the rest of the tape along the back. Repeat for the other side of the folder. Have the children decorate the messenger bags for their fathers or father-figures.

Option: Make a handle! With ten to twelve inches of tape, fold the tape over itself so the edges meet. Start in the middle of the length of tape and leave about two inches open at each end. Press the open ends to the top of the folder (on just one side) about three inches apart.

Bonus Activity

Teach children the old favorite "Rise and Shine" by playing a recording or singing the song for them. Invite them to wave their Sunshine Plates as they sing.

Saying Goodbye

Give the children their Sunshine Plates and their Messenger Bags.

Say: God created the sun and the earth. Today we celebrated the sun. Hooray for the sun!

If you made Messenger Bags, say a word about dads, too!

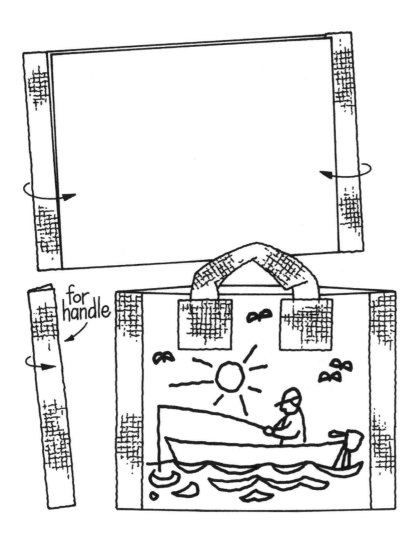

Bible Verse

[God] provides rain over the earth's surface, sends water to the open country.
(Job 5:10)

Supplies

- Garden pot
- Small umbrella or representation of an umbrella

Note

This story would be great when told with puppets, if you have them available.

Pray

God of Seedtime and Harvest, you have blessed our world with clouds and the rain they bring. Thanks for water and all the ways we enjoy it in our lives. Amen.

Plants Need Rain

Message:

Clouds and rain are part of God's creation.

Greeting with a Garden Pot

Put a small umbrella or a representation of an umbrella in the Garden Pot.

Greet the children. Choose a child to reach into the garden pot to reveal the umbrella. Invite the child or the group to name the object.

Say: We might want to keep our clothes and hair dry with an umbrella or rain coat, but the world needs the water that comes from raindrops. Plant life, people, and other living creatures must have water. Clouds and rain are an important part of God's creation.

Getting Set for the Story

Ask: Have you ever heard or seen a weather report on the radio or TV? What can a weather report tell us?

Explain that for today's story, the children will hear a pretend forecast from Mr. Puddle-mud, the TV meteorologist, who studies the weather, and Ms. Smilesalot, the news reporter.

Telling the Story

"And now it's time for the weather report with our Chief Meteorologist, Mr. Puddle-mud," said Ms. Smilesalot.

"Thank you, Ms. Smilesalot, and good evening, folks. Today we enjoyed a sunny, dry day with normal temperatures. This afternoon, we saw some clouds drifting in our beautiful blue sky. Tomorrow, you can expect a change in the weather. You'll see the first raindrops around sunrise and then as you go out to school or work or camp, the rain will be steadily coming down. Get out your rain gear! Everyone will see at least a half inch of rainfall. Some areas might see up to one inch of rain."

"Mr. Puddle-mud," asked Ms. Smilesalot, "will everyone receive rain?"

"Yes, this storm system will really help all our farmers and gardeners. They haven't had any rain in six weeks. This has hurt the plants in the fields and dried up the pasture grass for cows, sheep, and other animals."

"And the water in lakes and streams has fallen too," added Ms. Smilesalot.

"You're right, Ms. Smilesalot. Lots of rain soaks into the soil, and the water that doesn't go into the soil runs off into ponds, lakes, streams, and rivers."

"In my reporting," said Ms. Smilesalot, "I've learned that factories and businesses need and use a great deal of water too. We must have water for the places we work, for our homes, and for the foods we eat."

"That's true," answered Mr. Puddle-mud. "Sometimes we're grumpy when we find out that it's going to rain, but our world needs rainwater. So tomorrow, be thankful for the wonderful water the clouds will bring us!"

"Thanks, Mr. Puddle-mud. I'll carry my umbrella tomorrow!" said Ms. Smilesalot.

Exploring

Play the Sun or Shower Shuffle game to think about predicting the weather.

Prepare a deck of weather cards: Five sunny cards, each with a drawing of the sun; five cloudy cards, each with a drawing of a cloud; and five rainy cards, each with a drawing of rain drops.

Say: Even though meteorologists study the weather and try to tell us what to expect, the weather is very changeable and can surprise us all. Let's play a game.

Hand three blank index cards to each child. Set out the crayons. Show the children the cards you made, one at a time, and ask them to make their own copies.

Have the children put their own weather cards in front of them. Choose a child to guess which of the three kinds of weather is coming, pick up that card, and hold it high in the air. This is what the "meteorologist" predicts.

Now shuffle your own fifteen cards, lay them face-down, and have the child pick one to see what actually happened. See if the meteorologist got it right. Repeat, allowing each child a turn.

Celebrating with Music

Teach the children "Rain Clouds Go Marching," set to the tune of "The Ants Go Marching."

More Exploring

Try this easy Soak In or Run Off Experiment to observe how water can soak into or run off soil. You'll need one cup of ground soil or potting soil and one cup of water.

Pour the soil in the middle of the bowl. Make a small crater in the top of the pile of soil. Have a child dip the teaspoon into the water. Pour the spoonful of water into the crater. Taking turns, have the children put one spoonful of water on the soil and watch it soak in. Count how many teaspoons you can add before the water runs off.

Bonus Activity

Lead the children in an add-on prayer for rain. Explain that you will begin and that each child will add to the prayer by saying the name of a fruit, vegetable, plant, or tree.

Pray: Dear God, we ask that you send rain to water *(children fill in)*. We thank you for rain! Amen.

Saying Goodbye

Let children take the Sun and Shower cards home if they wish.

Say: Keep your eyes on the skies this week, as you look for rain clouds to bring us the water we need.

Supplies
- Index cards
- Crayons

Rain clouds go marching three by three, hoorah, hoorah.
Rain clouds go marching three by three, hoorah, hoorah.
Rain clouds go marching three by three, over the land and over the sea.
And we all know clouds are part of God's creation.

Supplies
- Soil
- Water
- Cup
- Bowl
- Teaspoon

Observe the Harvest Festival for the early produce of your crops that you planted in the field. (Exodus 23:16)

- Garden pot
- Vegetable

A Time to Harvest

Message:
We celebrate the harvest.

Greeting with a Garden Pot
Select a common vegetable and place it in the garden pot.

Greet the children. Hold up the garden pot.

Ask: My favorite garden vegetable is (*name*). What is your favorite vegetable? What is your favorite fruit?

Choose a child to reach into the garden pot to reveal the vegetable. Invite the children or the group to name the vegetable.

Say: When seeds sprout and become plants, and the plants are fully grown, they make vegetables and fruits. When these vegetables and fruits are ripe, or ready to eat, we pick them. The time when we pick them is called the "harvest." In Bible days, a celebration was held when the first fruits and vegetables were harvested. Today, we're going to celebrate this harvest.

Getting Set for the Story
The story features a Kids' Tasting Day at the farmer's market. As you read the story, include your children's names where indicated. If you have a small group, repeat the names. If your group is large, double up on names.

Telling the Story
"Here we are at the Kids' Tasting Day at the Farmer's Market," said Mr. Applegate. "We're going to enjoy the fresh flavors of the harvest. These fruits and vegetables were grown in local fields and gardens. Kids, let's stay together as we visit the different fruit and vegetable stands."

The Strawberry Fields Stand had small and large baskets of bright red berries on shelves. Two tables were spread with big, shiny strawberries, each on its own napkin. Everyone in the group tasted them.

(*Children's names*) decided to visit the Pea Pickin' Patch next. The farmer said he had some fun peas for them to try. "They're called sugar snaps. You eat the whole pea pod."

"They're snappy and sweet," said (*children's names*).

(*Children's names*) led the group to Carrots R Us. The kids saw white carrots, yellow carrots, red carrots, orange carrots, and purple carrots. The carrots had long fern-like tops, and they were tied into bunches. The farmer had a table with slices of different carrots on plates. "Yum," said (*children's names*). "These carrots are really crunchy and sweet."

Next the group went to the Rainbow Tomato Stand. "Wow," said (*children's names*). There are pink ones, yellow ones, green ones, red ones, purple ones, striped ones, and orange ones. Are they all tomatoes?"

"Yes," said the farmer. "They each have a tomato flavor, but some are sweeter or tangier. I've cut slices of the different tomatoes for you to try."

"Thanks," said (*children's names*). "These are delicious."

"Come on over to the Blueberry Hill," called a farmer.

Small cups of round blueberries were lined up on a table for the kids. "The first berry I ate was super sweet, but the second one was sweet and sour," said *(children's names)*.

"They're both good," said Mr. Applegate.

"Hey, this tasting is for kids," joked *(children's names)*.

(Children's names) said, "Let's see what's at Jill's Juice Stand." On the counter were small cups of freshly juiced fruits and vegetables. Jill gave the group samples of strawberry carrot juice, triple tomato juice, and pure blueberry juice. "This is fun," said *(children's names)*.

"Thank you for bringing us to the farmer's market, Mr. Applegate!"

Exploring
Provide a Farmer's Market Tasting for the children to experience and discuss. Select seasonal foods if possible.

Some groceries have vegetables and fruits pre-sliced and ready to eat. If you buy whole produce, wash and cut it into bite-size pieces. Place each in its own storage bag. Children may enjoy taking home leftovers, so bring additional storage bags.

Say: The Bible tells us to celebrate the harvest of the crops. You're about to taste two kinds of vegetables and two kinds of fruit.

Celebrating with Music
Teach the children "All Things Bright and Beautiful" by playing a recording or singing the song for them.

More Exploring
Play Garden Charades to show the steps from planting to harvest.

Make up enough actions that each child has a chance to act one out.

Explain that everyone will have a turn acting out something a gardener does. Whisper the clue to each player. (You can also write out the clues on note cards or paper slips if you choose.) For example, you might use putting on garden gloves, digging with a shovel, pulling weeds, planting seeds, watering, looking for seed sprouts, showing how big or tall a plant has grown, harvesting or picking vegetables from the plants.

Bonus Activity
Invite a gardener or a farmer from your area to visit the group. Ask the guest to tell what he or she grows, and let the children ask questions. Hopefully your visitor will bring along some edible visual aids!

Saying Goodbye
Give the children any food you have bagged for them from the Farmer's Market Tasting.

Say: God gave us seedtime and harvest. We're glad to know more about gardeners and farmers who help bring us the food we need and enjoy!

Pray
God of Seedtime and Harvest, like the kids in the story, we're happy to see and taste the harvest of vegetables and fruits. We ask your blessing on the food we are about to receive. Amen.

Supplies
- Two kinds of vegetables
- Two kinds of fruit
- Napkins
- Storage bags
- Juice or water and cups (optional)

All things bright and beautiful,
All creatures great and small,
All things wise and wonderful,
The Lord God made them all.

The cold wind in the winter,
The pleasant summer sun,
The ripe fruits in the garden,
God made them every one.

All things bright and beautiful,
All creatures great and small,
All things wise and wonderful,
The Lord God made them all.

Water Wonder

Bible Verse

You will be like a watered garden, like a spring of water that won't run dry.
(Isaiah 58:11)

Supplies

- Unbreakable beverage cup
- Paper
- Scissors

Like a Spring of Water

Message:

God wants us to open our hearts to feed the hungry.

Greeting with a Cup

Cut a simple heart from paper. Fold the heart and place it in the cup.

Greet the children. Hold up the cup.

Ask: Why do we use this? What is your favorite thing to drink?

Choose a child to reach into the cup to discover what's inside. Have the child unfold the heart and show it to everyone.

Say: A heart like this reminds us of love, kindness, and giving.

Ask: Where is your heart? Can you think of a time when your heart felt happy because you were kind or giving?

Say: It's good when we are kind and giving to our friends and family, but God also wants us to open our hearts to people we don't even know who need our help.

Getting Set for the Story

Share these words from Isaiah 58:10-11 by reading a phrase and then repeating it with the children. (The wording has been simplified to make the passage easier for children to understand.)

> If you open your heart *(repeat)* to the hungry *(repeat)*, and give to the needy *(repeat)*, your light will shine *(repeat)* in the darkness *(repeat)*, and your gloom *(repeat)* will be like the noon. *(repeat)* The LORD will guide you always *(repeat)* and give to you *(repeat)*, even in parched places. *(repeat)*

> You will be *(repeat)* like a watered garden *(repeat)*, like a spring of water *(repeat)* that never runs dry." *(repeat)*

Say: This Bible passage tells us that if we open our hearts to the hungry and the needy, as God wants us to do, then God will help us. The children in our story will learn about a food bank and find ways to help the hungry.

Telling the Story

Mrs. Goodall asked, "Have you seen people bringing grocery bags and boxes of food into the church?" The kids nodded their heads as Caroline asked, "Are we going to have a big supper and invite a lot of people?"

Mrs. Goodall answered, "We do invite visitors to come to our suppers, but the food we're collecting is going to the food bank in our area."

"What's a food bank?" asked Mckenzie.

"Good question," said Mrs. Goodall. "It's a place that gives groceries to people who don't have enough food for their family. When grownups lose their jobs or get injured or really sick, they may miss work and not have enough money for food."

"So the food bank feeds hungry people?" asked Alden.

"Being hungry makes your tummy hurt," said Caroline.

"Yes," agreed Mrs. Goodall. "That's why the food bank needs donations of food."

"What kind of food do families need?" asked Kyra.

"They need breakfast!" said Mckenzie. "Like cereal and milk, eggs and bread, peanut butter and jelly, or fruit and cheese."

"And people need lunch," added Celeste. "Soup and all the stuff you need for sandwiches, crunchy veggies, and fruit cups."

"Don't forget supper," said Alex. "I like spaghetti with lots of sauce and tacos with salsa and chili and cheese on top. It takes all kinds of jars and cans and bags to make supper."

"The food bank needs foods for breakfast, lunch, and supper so people won't be hungry," said Mrs. Goodall.

"How can we help?" asked Angela.

"We're on our way to the fellowship hall," said Mrs. Goodall, "to sort the boxes, cans, bottles, jars, and bags people in our church have brought in."

The kids were ready to work. Mrs. Goodall led the group as they emptied the bags and put the cereals in boxes, and the jars, cans, and cups of fruit in other boxes. The canned meats and fish were boxed up too, and the soups were stacked and packed. Rice, noodles, taco kits, and sauces were put in boxes along with lots of vegetables.

When the kids had counted and packed all the different kinds of food, Mrs. Goodall opened a big envelope. She pulled out a handful of money. "This money will buy food that needs to go in a refrigerator, like milk."

"I like helping," said Celeste.

"What else can we do?" asked Matthew.

"Mrs. Goodall said, "We can decorate posters to remind people to donate food or we can decorate bags for people to put their food donations in. God wants us to open our hearts to the hungry."

Pray

God of Wonder, we pray that you will open the hearts of many people, so they will help the hungry be healthy. Let our giving be like a spring of water that never runs dry. Amen.

Supplies

- Paper grocery bags
- Manila folders
- Crayons
- Construction paper
- Glue
- Scissors

God is so good,
God is so good,
God is so good,
is so good to me.

God sends the rain … sends
the rain to us.

Rain waters plants … waters
plants for us.

Supplies

- Cups
- Pitcher
- Drinking water

Exploring

Encourage others to donate to the local food bank, shelter, or soup kitchen. Have the children decorate Food Donation Bags or make Donation Posters from manila folders. (If time permits, you may want to have them do both.) Food Donation Bags may be sent home with the children or kept for distribution at church. Donation Posters should be hung at church.

Suggest that those decorating Donation Bags cut construction paper hearts to glue over the store logo, following the theme of "Open your hearts to the hungry." Or, children may simply color the bags.

For Donation Posters, the manila folders should be opened and laid flat. Suggest that the posters follow the "Watered Garden" theme, showing fruits, vegetables, and other plants growing in a garden. These posters could read: "Be like a garden! Give food to_____" (fill in the name of the collection/organization). Children may color their posters and also use construction paper and glue if you choose.

Say: A watered garden brings forth beautiful, healthy plants. Some of these plants produce vegetables and fruit for people to eat. When we open our hearts to help people who are hungry, we are like a watered garden too!

Celebrating with Music

Read the Bible verse to the children. Then sing "God Is So Good" by playing a recording or by singing the song to the children. Encourage the children to make up words using some of the ideas from the Bible verse.

More Exploring

Say: We've been learning about sharing food with the hungry, but the Bible tells us that it's also good to share water. Listen: "Everybody who gives even a cup of cold water to these little ones … will certainly be rewarded" (Matthew 10:42).

Say: In Bible times, there were no kitchen or bathroom water faucets. People had to go out and get their water. Giving someone a cup of cold water was a real gift of kindness, because drinking water was hard to find.

Have the children watch as you pour each of them a cup of cold water. Place a cup of water before each child, but ask them to wait for your instructions. Then tell them to carefully give their own cup to the person on their right, saying, "We are like springs of water!" Enjoy the drink.

Bonus Activity

Invite a guest to speak to the children about hunger relief in your community. Recruit a food bank or Meals on Wheels volunteer.

Saying Goodbye

If the children are taking Food Donation Bags home, give these out now, with any instructions.

Say: Thank you for opening your hearts to the hungry as God wants us to do. You are like a spring of water!

Jesus in the Jordan River

Message:
Jesus believes in baptism.

Greeting with a Cup
Ahead of time, fill the cup with water.

Greet the children. Hold up the cup. Invite the children to each dip a finger in the water.

Say: It's fun to play in water, but water has more important purposes too. Many cities and towns get their drinking water from a river. Their water treatment buildings are nearby, so the river water can be cleaned and made ready for people to drink. Rivers have been important sources of water for thousands of years. Years ago, people went to the river to get water for drinking, cooking, and washing, and to use for their work. Some baptisms took place in rivers, and today, some people are still baptized in rivers. Let's hear about a river baptism in the Bible, the baptism of Jesus.

Getting Set for the Story
Say: The word "baptize" is a very old word, which comes from the Greek language. The Greek word, *baptizein*, sounds almost the same as what we say, and it means to "dip in water." Baptism is a ceremony that says we are children of God.

Discuss how baptisms are done at your church.

Say: Jesus believed in baptism. Listen to a story about his baptism in a river. When I hold up a finger, we'll all say, "Jesus believes in baptism."

Telling the Story
A man known as John the Baptist was in the desert. He called out to everyone: "Change your hearts and lives! Here comes the kingdom of heaven!"

Then John the Baptist went to the Jordan River to baptize those who wanted to change their hearts. People came from all over the area to hear him speak and to be baptized. But John said the people must first tell the unkind or wrong things they had done. John also said they must be sorry and decide not to do the wrong things anymore. Then he baptized them in the river.

John the Baptist told the people that someone was coming after him, a person who was strong, a person who could baptize them with the Holy Spirit. That person was Jesus.

About that time, Jesus came from Galilee to the Jordan River, and asked John to baptize him, too.

JESUS BELIEVES IN BAPTISM.

John was surprised: "I need to be baptized by you, yet you come to me."

JESUS BELIEVES IN BAPTISM.

Jesus answered him, "Allow me to be baptized now. This is what God wants." So John agreed to baptize Jesus in the Jordan River.

Bible Verse
A voice from heaven said, "This is my Son whom I dearly love; I find happiness in him." (Matthew 3:17)

Supplies
- Unbreakable beverage cup
- Water

God of Wonder, we thank you for John the Baptist, who baptized Jesus. We praise you for the wonder of your Spirit and your voice that blessed Jesus. Amen.

Supplies

- #4 cone coffee filters
- Tape
- Crayons (optional)

JESUS BELIEVES IN BAPTISM.

When Jesus was baptized, he looked up and saw the Spirit of God coming down like a dove resting on him. A voice from heaven said, "This is my Son whom I dearly love; I find happiness in him."

JESUS BELIEVES IN BAPTISM.

Exploring

Make a dove—a symbol of Jesus' baptism. Each dove takes four filters. Make a sample to show the children.

To form the body, roll a coffee filter into a tight cone, with the crimped end of the filter making a point. Wrap the point with tape to secure the dove's beak. Next, tape along the seam. Since children will play with the doves, make sure they are taped securely.

The tail is formed by curving the crimped end of another coffee filter and sliding it into the open end of the body about an inch. Tape each side of the tail to the cone body.

To create the wings, tape two filters together at the crimped ends. Lay the wings over the body, between the beak and tail. Tape the underside of the wing to the body of the dove on each side.

Say: To remember Jesus' baptism, we're going to make doves.

Show the children your sample, and then distribute the coffee filters (four per child). If you wish, have each child color a filter for the body. You can roll and tape these while the children color the wings and tail. Have them put their initials on the doves. Assemble the doves.

Show children how the doves' wings flap when waved through the air.

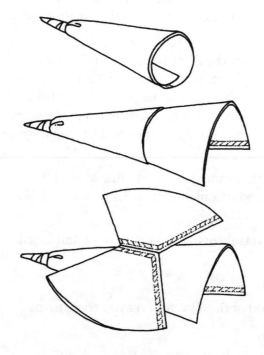

Celebrating with Music

Teach children "I've Got Peace Like a River" by playing a recording or singing the song for them.

More Exploring

Learn more about John the Baptist and enjoy a treat.

Say: John the Baptist and Jesus were cousins. The angel Gabriel came to Jesus' mother and father and also to John's father and announced that each would be born and what their names would be.

Say: When he grew up, John lived in the wilderness. He dressed in clothes made of camel's hair with a leather belt around his waist. He ate locusts and wild honey. By teaching and baptizing, John prepared the way for Jesus, who is the Messiah.

Share a taste of honey with the children by squirting a bit on their spoons. Serve seconds if the children would like to taste more honey. If you have graham crackers or bread, serve some honey this way.

You may choose to serve water or juice with the honey and bread.

Bonus Activity

Share photos of family baptisms, a baptismal outfit, or another memento. Consider e-mailing parents ahead of time, asking them to please send in baptismal photos and/or sweet and funny stories.

Saying Goodbye

Give the children the doves they made. Invite them to gently flap the dove's wings.

Say: This week, let your doves remind you of Jesus' baptism in the river. Jesus believes in baptism!

I've got peace like a river,
I've got peace like a river,
I've got peace like a river in
my soul. [Repeat]

Supplies

- Honey in a squirt bottle
- Spoons
- Graham crackers or bread (optional)
- Napkins

"Come, follow me," he said, "and I'll show you how to fish for people." (Mark 1:17)

Supplies
- Unbreakable beverage cup
- Paper
- Scissors or crayon

Supplies
- Bible

Pray

God of Wonder, you loved the world so much that you sent your Son, Jesus, to teach us, lead us, and save us. We will invite people to church so they can know your love through Jesus too. Amen.

Follow Me by the Sea

Message:

We can invite people to church.

Greeting with a Cup

Introduce the message by presenting a cup with a paper fish inside. Cut out a simple fish or draw one on paper. Fold the fish and put it in the cup.

Greet the children. Hold up the cup.

Choose a child to reach into the cup to discover the paper fish. Ask the child to show everyone the fish.

Say: People have been fishing for thousands of years with a pole and bait, with nets, or with clever traps made of sticks, grass, and other materials. Some people fish from the water's edge. Others fish in boats or from bridges or piers. Some people wade right into the water.

Getting Set for the Story

Say: Listen to what the Bible says about how Jesus found his first disciples.

Read Mark 1:16-20.

Say: Jesus wanted to gather a group of disciples to learn about his message and help with his ministry. He fished for people by preaching, teaching, healing, and working miracles. After a while, crowds of people came to see and hear him. His disciples learned how to ask others to follow him. That's how they fished for people too. In our story, we'll hear how children in a church fished for people by inviting them to church.

Telling the Story

"It's a great day for our church picnic," said Gabe. "Could we invite Nick and Ray to come with us?"

Gabe's father asked, "Why don't we invite the whole family? I'll call them."

"No, Dad," said Gabe. "I want to invite them."

Gabe called their house. He told his friends there would be games, swimming, hiking, and plenty of food. Nick and Ray's family said they'd like to come, and they'd bring a big watermelon and a soccer ball.

Claire wanted to invite her friend Ellie to sleep over at her house. Claire's mom said, "Yes, she may spend the night. Ask Ellie if she'd like to go to Sunday school with you. I'm teaching tomorrow."

Ellie's mom took her to Claire's house. Ellie brought pink pajamas and an outfit for church.

At the worship service, Grayson noticed that a new family was visiting. He introduced himself and told them he was a Children's Church helper. Grayson invited the two kids to go with him to Children's Church. The kids gave him big smiles.

During the announcements on Sunday, the pastor thanked Gabe, Claire, Grayson, and all the kids who had invited others to come to church activities. "Jesus wants us to fish for people," he said. "Good job!"

Exploring

Make Funny Fish to remember that Jesus wants us to fish for people. Make a sample fish. Cut a four-inch triangle into the rim of the plate. This opening forms the mouth, and the triangle cutout is the tail piece. Tape or staple the tail opposite the mouth, extending from the other side of the plate with the point of the triangle facing in.

Prepare the plates for the children by penciling the cutting lines for the triangle or by cutting out the triangles ahead of time.

Show the children the Funny Fish. Set out the supplies. If the children are cutting their own triangle fins, ask them to do this now. Next, have them tape or staple on the fins. Invite the children to color the fish with any colors or patterns they choose.

When the Funny Fish are finished, ask the children to form a semi-circle, holding their fish. Tell them their fish are now part of a school of fish.

Say: I'll pick a leader. The leader will make her or his fish swim a certain way. Then you will all copy the leader and make your fish swim that way too!

Let each child take a turn leading the school of fish.

Celebrating with Music

Teach children the second verse of "Peace Like a River" by playing a recording or singing the song for them.

More Exploring

Play a Greeting Game to learn how to welcome visitors. Demonstrate the greeting by extending your right hand to shake with a child, saying, "Hi, my name is *(fill in name)*. Welcome!"

Put the children in groups of two. If your children vary in age, it's a good idea to pair older with younger ones. Have them take turns pretending they are welcoming someone to church.

Say: It's important to help our visitors and new members feel welcome.

Bonus Activity

Make Fishy Postcards using index cards and markers. Your pastor or church outreach committee can mail the cards to visitors and new members.

Have the children color a fish on the blank side of the index card. Explain that the card will go in the mail to welcome someone who visited or just joined the church.

Saying Goodbye

Hand out the Funny Fish.

Say: Jesus told his disciples to fish for people. We can fish for people by inviting people to church activities and by making them feel welcome when they're here.

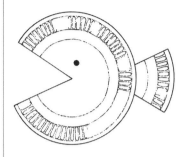

I've got love like an ocean,
I've got love like an ocean,
I've got love like an ocean in my soul. [Repeat]

[If you wish, teach the third verse, as well.]

I've got joy like a fountain,
I've got joy like a fountain,
I've got joy like a fountain in my soul. [Repeat]

Supplies

- Index cards (4 x 6 inches)
- Washable markers

God created the great sea animals and all the tiny living things that swarm in the waters, each according to its kind. (Genesis 1:21)

Supplies

- Unbreakable beverage cup
- Paper
- Crayons

Supplies

- #4 cone coffee filters
- Yarn or ribbon
- Scissors
- Stapler or tape

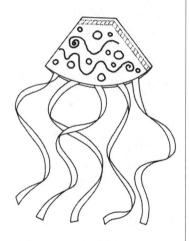

Pray

God of Wonder, we marvel at the amazing sea animals that live in the pools along the beach and in the deepest trenches in the ocean. Help us understand the importance of the sea and its creatures. Amen.

God's Great Sea Animals

Message:
God created wonderful sea animals.

Greeting with a Cup
Draw a simple picture of a sea animal such as a jellyfish, octopus, or whale. Place the picture in the cup, folding if necessary.

Greet the children. Hold up the cup. Choose a child to reach in the cup to discover what's inside and show everyone the picture. Read the Bible verse.

Say: All the sizes, colors, shapes, and types of sea animals are a wonder of God's creation!

Getting Set for the Story
Children will follow the story with Jellyfish Hand Puppets.

Prepare the puppets ahead of time. Tape or staple five twelve-inch lengths of yarn or ribbon to the inside rim of a coffee filter. These are the tentacles of the jellyfish. Children will decorate their puppets later. Prepare a puppet for each child.

Say: Here come some wiggly jellyfish!

Give everyone a Jellyfish Hand Puppet to slip on. Have the children pretend their jellyfish are floating on the waves (gentle bobbing hand motions), turning (turn hand back and forth), or swimming back out to sea (tip the puppet forward and move slowly).

Say: During the story, let your jellyfish move to the actions you hear.

Telling the Story
John and Julie Jellyfish floated on the gently rolling waves. Up and down, up and down, they bobbed. Their bodies jiggled and shimmered in the noonday sunshine.

Their long tentacles hung below the water, touching things that drifted or swam by. They liked to catch small fish and clusters of fish eggs to eat.

As the afternoon went by, a pod of dolphins swam near John and Julie. The dolphins played and jumped in the waves as they traveled.

Many miles at sea, a humpback whale sang a long song to her family that vibrated through the waters. Did the jellyfish feel the music?

A school of bluefish passed below John and Julie's tentacles. Later, a few red snapper fish hurried by as the sky became dark and cloudy.

Rain tapped the water, and the winds pushed at the waves, making them white-capped and choppy. The jellyfish were swirled and smacked by the wild waves. Night came and the storm churned the sea.

John and Julie Jellyfish sensed they were getting close to the beach. Under them, a flounder snuggled into the sand, with one eye looking up. Nearby, a crab scuttled under the sand too. The waves carried lots of shells up onto the beach.

John and Julie felt odd things float through their tentacles. A board, some plastic bottles, aluminum cans, a torn net, and a tire floated by them.

The next morning the storm was gone. John and Julie Jellyfish were still safe in the seawater under a pier. If they had been tossed up on the beach by the stormy sea, they might have died.

The jellyfish swam slowly with the outgoing tide, so they could be farther out to sea. After catching a breakfast of tiny minnow fish, John and Julie Jellyfish went even farther out into the sea.

Exploring
Say: Let's give John and Julie Jellyfish some color!

Set out crayons. Let the children color the Jellyfish Hand Puppets any way they like. Have them write their names on the backs of the puppets.

Celebrating with Music
Teach children "Who Did Swallow Jonah" by playing a recording or singing the song for them.

More Exploring
Color Squiggly Eels in honor of the eels of the Sargasso Sea. If you can, bring in photographs of eels from a book or the internet to share.

Say: In the Atlantic Ocean, there is an unusual area called the Sargasso Sea. Four ocean currents form the borders, and inside the currents the waters are calmer and clearer. The American eel lays and hatches its eggs in the Sargasso Sea. The baby eels grow bigger and stronger until they can swim to the East Coast of the United States, where they finish growing. When the eels become adults, they swim all the way back to the Sargasso Sea.

Say: While the Sargasso Sea protects swarms of tiny sea animals, it also collects trash. The currents carry plastic bags, bottles, and other items along their paths and leave them in the Sargasso Sea. Because we respect God's water wonders, we want to keep all trash out of streams, rivers, ponds, lakes, bays, and oceans.

Say: Let's make Squiggly Eels in honor of the eels that hatch and return to the Sargasso Sea!

Show the children pictures of eels if you have them, but tell them they can decorate their Squiggly Eels any way they want. Point out that some varieties of eels have spots! Give each child a piece of paper and set out the crayons.

Bonus Activity
Share books based on sea creatures. Three favorites are *Swimmy* by Leo Lionni, *Mister Seahorse* by Eric Carle, and *The Rainbow Fish* by Marcus Pfister.

Saying Goodbye
Hand out the Jellyfish Hand Puppets and the Squiggly Eel pictures.

Say: God made the oceans good. Let's help keep them good!

Who did (who did), Who did (who did), Who did swallow Jo, Jo, Jo, Jo?
Who did (who did), Who did (who did), Who did swallow Jo, Jo, Jo, Jo?
Who did (who did), Who did (who did), Who did swallow Jo, Jo, Jo, Jo?
Who did swallow Jonah?
Who did swallow Jonah?
Who did swallow Jonah down?
[Repeat with "Whale did."]

Supplies
- Paper
- Crayons
- Photos of eels (optional)

Color Joy

Bible Verse

They should make me a sanctuary so I can be present among them.
(Exodus 25:8)

Supplies

- Box of crayons

A Beautiful Tabernacle

Message:

God wants to be among us.

Greeting with a Crayon Box

Introduce the message by presenting a crayon box.

Greet the children. Hold up the crayon box.

Ask: Have you ever used all the colors in a crayon box?

Say: Today we'll see lots of colors during our story, which is about a colorful tent.

Ask: Have you ever made or put up a tent?

Say: When the Israelites followed God away from Egypt and into the wilderness, they camped in tents as they traveled. Their leader, Moses, pitched a special tent outside the camp. The tent was a place to worship God. Although this tent had a special purpose, it wasn't really fancy.

Ask: Can you think of any fancy colored tents you've seen?

Say: Even though we live thousands of years later than Moses, we still use and see tents. Fancy, multi-colored tents are used at weddings and outdoor parties, at fairs and festivals, and at markets and stores.

Getting Set for the Story

As you tell the story, use a box of crayons to show the children the colors of the Tabernacle. An assortment of crayons that includes gold and bronze adds to the intrigue but isn't necessary.

Say: Some time after God gave Moses the Ten Commandments, God told Moses to build a big fancy tent. The tent would be a place to be with God and to worship God. This new tent was called the Tabernacle.

Telling the Story

God spoke to Moses and told him many things were needed to build the big Tabernacle, supply it with furnishings, and provide clothing for the priests. God said the Tabernacle would be made from the offerings of the people. God wanted these offerings to be given willingly, from the heart.

God told Moses to collect these materials: Gold *(Show gold or yellow crayon.)*; bronze *(Show bronze or orange crayon.)*; blue, purple, and red yarns *(Show blue, purple, and red crayons.)*; fine linen cloth and goat's hair *(Show white or beige crayon.)*; ram's skins dyed red *(Show red crayon.)*; tanned leather and acacia wood *(Show brown crayon)*; oil for lamps; spices for anointing oil and incense; onyx stone *(Show black crayon.)*; and jewels for the vest of the high priest. *(Show green, blue, purple, and red crayons.)*

Then God told Moses, "Make me a sanctuary so I can be present among my people." And the people used the materials they had collected to make a tent in which to worship God.

Next, God gave directions for building the ark, a special box that would hold the Ten Commandments: "Make a box of acacia wood *(Show brown crayon)* and cover it inside and out with gold. *(Show gold or yellow crayon.)* Make gold molding around the box and four gold rings to put on the four feet of the box. *(Show gold or yellow crayon.)* Make two acacia wood poles to go through the rings, so the ark may be carried. *(Show brown crayon.)* Put the stone tablets of the Ten Commandments in the ark. *(Show gray crayon.)* Next, build a cover of pure gold *(Show gold or yellow crayon.)* and decorate it with two statues of cherubs with wings in gold.

God had many instructions and plans for every part of the big tent. Moses listened to God and did exactly as God wished, with the help of the people.

Exploring
Children will fashion a simple Tabernacle Tent, focusing on the entrance, the cloth hangings, and the ark.

Prepare a folder for each child. First, trim off the tab. Next, lay the folder in front of you horizontally, with the fold at the top. At the bottom, measure six inches from one edge to the center. Make a pencil mark. Next, use scissors to cut straight up about six inches from the pencil mark toward the top.

Finish each folder by creating triangular tent flaps. Lift and turn back a triangle from each side of the six-inch slit. This will show a bit of the interior of the tent. Crease the folds.

Give the children the prepared folders and crayons.

Say: Here's a tabernacle for you to decorate. You will begin by coloring the tent flaps blue, red, and purple. The Bible says the curtains had blue edges and were very beautiful.

Have the children color the tent flaps.

Next, ask them to open their folder. Have them draw a box in the middle of the bottom portion of the folder.

Say: This is the ark that held the Ten Commandments. It was made of wood and covered with sheets of gold. It's a very holy piece in the Tabernacle. Use a yellow or gold crayon to color it.

Have the children color the ark. They may outline it in a darker color if they like.

Say: Finally, it's time to color the inside veil or curtains of the Tabernacle. The curtains were blue, purple, and red, with blue edges. Draw curtains

Pray
Creator of Colors, your Tabernacle was a sanctuary and our church is a sanctuary, too. We're glad you want to be with us as we worship, and we like seeing your beautiful colors at church and in the world around us. Amen.

Supplies
- Manila folders
- Crayons
- Scissors
- Rulers
- Pencil

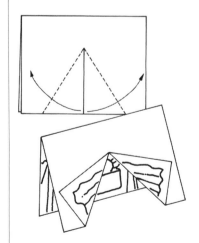

Kum ba yah, my Lord,
kum ba yah.
Kum ba yah, my Lord,
kum ba yah.
Kum ba yah, my Lord,
kum ba yah.
Oh Lord, kum ba yah.

Someone's crying, Lord,
kum ba yah...

Someone's laughing, Lord,
kum ba yah...

Someone's singing, Lord,
kum ba yah...

Someone's praying, Lord,
kum ba yah...

Supplies
- Spices
- Small containers

Supplies
- Applesauce
- Cinnamon sugar
- Spoons
- Cups

that hang from the top of the folder all the way to the bottom, on both sides of the ark.

Have the children set their folders upright like tents. Invite them to peek into one another's tabernacles.

Celebrating with Music
Teach children "Kum Ba Yah" by playing a recording or singing the song for them. Explain that "kum ba yah" means "come by here."

More Exploring
Children can imagine the fragrance of the Tabernacle by smelling spices. Select some of these spices: cinnamon, nutmeg, cloves, allspice, anise, or combinations such as pumpkin pie spice or mulling spices. Pour a bit of each selection in a small container. Plan to pass these containers around the group for everyone to sniff.

Say: The Tabernacle was also called the "Tent of Meeting" because people went there to worship and to meet God. The Israelites believed that God enjoyed pleasing smells, so the Tabernacle smelled good inside. We're going to smell some of the spices they might have put into oil or used to make incense.

Pass the spices around one at a time and tell the name of each one. As the children sniff it, ask if they have ever smelled the spice before.

Say: Thanks to God for the sense of smell and the sense of taste. They add spice to life!

Bonus Activity
Make an easy snack by sprinkling cinnamon sugar on applesauce or buying cinnamon applesauce cups. Point out that spices that are used to make candles, incense, potpourri, soaps, and lotions can sometimes be used to flavor food. One of those spices is cinnamon.

Saying Goodbye
Hand out the Tabernacle Tents.

Say: Enjoy playing with your tents at home. Remember that God is with us!

Grassy Meadows

Message:
We feel safe in God's faithful love.

Bible Verse

He lets me rest in grassy meadows; he leads me to restful waters. (Psalm 23:2)

Supplies

• Box of crayons

Greeting with a Crayon Box
Introduce the message by presenting a crayon box.

Greet the children. Hold up the crayon box.

Ask: What color is new spring grass?

Choose a child to select a green crayon from the box and show the group.

Ask: Can you name some other plants in God's creation that are green?

Say: God's creation has lots of green plant life: in the frozen arctic, there is green algae; in the hot tropics, there are banana trees; in the farmlands, there are green-leaved vegetables and grains; in the swamp, there are green marsh grasses; in the mountains, there are evergreen trees; and in the desert, there are green cacti. God's green is everywhere!

Getting Set for the Story
After a bit of background on the Twenty-third Psalm, read and discuss the psalm verse by verse.

Say: One book in our Bible is Psalms. The Psalms are poems, and many were sung in the temples for Hebrew worship. One of the most famous and favorite psalms is the Twenty-third Psalm.

We believe that David wrote many of the psalms. David was a shepherd when he was a young man, and he played beautiful music for King Saul. Later, David became the King of Israel.

For our story, we'll read and talk about each verse of the Twenty-third Psalm. This beloved psalm helps us feel safe in God's love.

Telling the Story
Verse 1: "The LORD is my shepherd. I shall lack nothing."

Ask: How is God like a shepherd to us?

Say: A good shepherd watches over the sheep, protecting and caring for them. God is like a shepherd because God guides us, loves us, listens to our prayers, and cares for us when we are sad or troubled.

Verse 2: "He lets me rest in grassy meadows; he leads me to restful waters."

Ask: Why do sheep need grass and water?

Say: The Bible says that God is our shepherd and we are his sheep. Sheep need plenty of green meadow grass and calm, calm streams and pools to drink from. We may not eat meadow grass, but we do eat green-leaved vegetables, fruits, and grains. And we also need good water to drink.

Verse 3: "He keeps me alive. He guides me in proper paths for the sake of his good name."

Ask: Besides finding grass and water, why does a shepherd guide his sheep?

Say: A shepherd wants the sheep to know the right way to go each day. We, too, want to be on the right path so we don't get into trouble or hurt other people. When we are thinking about the right and proper thing to do, we can turn to God in prayer; we can talk to parents, teachers, or people in our church family; and we can listen to our own hearts.

Verse 4: "Even when I walk through the darkest valley, I fear no danger because you are with me. Your rod and your staff—they protect me."

Ask: When someone you like puts an arm around you, how does that feel?

Say: When someone puts an arm around us, we feel loved and safe. As our shepherd, God brings us love and comfort, even in sad or scary times.

Say: A shepherd's rod was used to protect the sheep from dangerous animals, like wolves. It was also used to count the sheep to see if any were missing. The staff, with a crook at one end, helped to gather the sheep or rescue a sheep from water or a rocky place.

Verse 5: "You set a table for me right in front of my enemies. You bathe my head in oil; my cup is so full it spills over!"

Ask: Have you ever poured a cup so full that it spilled over?

Say: This verse talks about the good things that God brings into our lives, such as a table of food prepared for us or a cup filled so generously it spills.

Ask: Does anyone know why our heads would be bathed with oil?

Say: Oil pressed from almonds, olives, or other plant life was very special in Bible times. Oil was poured on the heads of leaders or the sick. It was also poured on people as a sign of welcome or friendship. In this psalm, oil on the head is another sign of God's love.

Verse 6: "Yes, goodness and faithful love will pursue me all the days of my life, and I will live in the LORD's house as long as I live."

Ask: What days are your birthdays?

Say: Today's date is *(fill in date)*. You have already had many days in your life. There are 365 days in a year. The Twenty-third Psalm says that God's goodness and faithfulness will be with us all the days of our lives.

Exploring

The children will first pretend cotton balls are individual sheep and use chenille stems as rods to count out sheep. Then they will turn the chenille stems into Shepherd's Staffs to gather the sheep into a flock. Finally, they'll use the cotton balls to make Green Meadow Sheep.

Green construction paper makes a nice grassy field for this project. If you don't have green construction paper, color a green field on white paper.

Say: You're going to be shepherds counting and gathering your sheep!

Place the cotton balls within reach of the "shepherds." Give each child a chenille stem. Have them use the stem to count out ten cotton balls.

Show the children how to shape a chenille stem into a Shepherd's Staff by bending one end into a crook. Have them use their staffs to gather the sheep they counted.

Pray

Read each line of the Twenty-third Psalm again, and then ask the children to repeat that line with you. Conclude by praying, "Thank you, God, for your faithful love. Amen."

Supplies

- Cotton balls
- Chenille stems
- Green construction paper or white paper and a green crayon
- Glue
- Crayons

Give each child a sheet of green construction paper. (If you have white paper, invite them to color a grassy green meadow.)

Say: Let's make Green Meadow Sheep. Your paper is a grassy green meadow. In the meadow, you will make a sheep with your cotton balls.

On each child's sheet, squirt an oval of glue and then squiggle glue inside the oval. Have the children place their cotton balls inside the oval to make the body of a sheep. Ask them to color a nose and legs.

Say: Let your beautiful sheep remind you to feel safe in God's faithful love.

Have the children write names or initials on their Green Meadow Sheep. Set the pictures and the Shepherd's Staffs aside.

Celebrating with Music
Sing "Jesus Loves Me" by playing a recording or singing the song.

Say: In the Bible, Jesus says, "I am the good shepherd. I know my own sheep and they know me" (John 10:14). Let's sing of Jesus' faithful love.

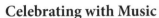

More Exploring
Treat the children to a Shepherd's Picnic.

Beforehand, wash grapes and cut the stems into small clusters. Section the pita bread if you are serving it. Prepare a plate for each child with grapes, cheese cubes, and crackers or bread. Fill the cups with water.

A green cloth, if you have one, can represent a grassy meadow. If you don't have a green cloth, bring another cloth that children can sit on.

Say: Because we feel safe in God's faithful love, we're going to rejoice with a shepherd's picnic!

Spread out the picnic cloth. If you have a green one, tell children this represents the green of a grassy meadow. Invite the children to sit, and then offer them the plates of food and cups of water.

Say: In Bible times, shepherds carried their food in a pouch, so they could eat while they kept watch over their sheep. Bread, cheese, and fruit made an easy and healthy meal.

While they are snacking, ask children to imagine what life as a shepherd in Bible times must have been like. Do you see any wolves on the horizon?

Bonus Activity
Invite one or more youth in the congregation to dress in robes and headscarves to become shepherds. They can join the picnic and perhaps act out a small skit for the children.

Saying Goodbye
Hand out the Green Meadow Sheep and the Shepherd's Staffs.

Say: The Lord is your shepherd. Feel safe in God's faithful love!

Jesus loves me, this I know,
for the Bible tells me so.
Little ones to him belong,
they are weak, but he is
strong.
Yes, Jesus loves me!
Yes, Jesus loves me!
Yes, Jesus loves me!
The Bible tells me so.

Supplies
- Green grapes
- Scissors
- Cheese cubes
- Crackers or pita bread
- Water
- Cups
- Plates
- Picnic cloth (preferably green)

As [Lydia] listened, the Lord enabled her to embrace Paul's message. (Acts 16:14)

Supplies
• Box of crayons

Supplies
• Map of Paul's Journeys

Pray
Creator of Colors, Paul, Silas, and Lydia all showed a strong faith in Jesus. We pray we will grow stronger in our faith and show our true colors as Christians. Amen.

Fancy Fabric

Message:
Our faith grows stronger as we learn more about Jesus.

Greeting with a Crayon Box
Greet the children. Hold up the crayon box. Pull out the purple crayon.

Ask: What color is this? Do you have any clothes made of purple cloth?

Say: When we shop for clothes, we have so many colors to choose from. In Bible times, certain colors, like purple, cost a lot of money. Rich people, government leaders, and church leaders wore purple cloth or clothes trimmed with purple yarn.

Say: A woman named Lydia was a dealer in purple cloth and probably also sold purple dyes and yarns. She was a businesswoman who might have worn purple clothes too. It is believed that Lydia was the first Christian convert in Europe.

Getting Set for the Story
Look for a map in your Bible, in a Bible dictionary or study guide, or on the internet that shows Paul's travels in the Mediterranean Sea countries.

Show the children the map. Point out the city of Jerusalem and the city of Philippi in Macedonia. Explain that Paul traveled the land and the sea to tell the good news of Jesus.

Telling the Story
The Apostle Paul and his companion Silas were traveling to bring the word of Jesus to people in other counties. The two arrived in Philippi.

They stayed several days in the city, but on the Sabbath, they went outside the city gate to find a quiet place to pray.

Soon, they found a river and looked for a place to sit on the riverbank. There, they met a group of women. One of the women was Lydia.

Paul talked to the women about the life and teachings of Jesus Christ. Paul shared his belief that Jesus was God's son, the Savior.

Lydia listened. She already believed in God, and Paul's message was powerful. God helped her understand Paul and believe in Jesus.

She was baptized by Paul in the river. Lydia brought everyone in her household to be baptized, also in the name of Jesus Christ.

Lydia, now baptized, invited Paul and Silas to be guests in her home for the rest of their time in Philippi.

Paul and Silas continued their travels to teach people about Jesus, but whenever they went back to Philippi, they stayed with Lydia and found encouragement from their brothers and sisters of faith in Jesus.

Exploring
To honor Lydia, children will make Fancy Fabric Prints.

You will need one half sheet of paper for each child. If you can find purple paper, this fits nicely for an activity related to Lydia.

Collect paint color sample cards from paint stores or paint departments. You'll need about four cards per child. Most stores will be glad for you to take some paint cards for a children's project.

Say: Lydia sold purple cloth. Cloth often has a print or pattern on it, such as checks, polka dots, stripes, flowers, or squares that make a plaid. We're going to make our own Fancy Fabric Prints.

Hand out supplies. Invite the children to cut the sample cards into shapes and move the shapes around on the paper until they make something they like. Then they can glue the shapes in place.

Say: Let your Fancy Fabric Prints remind you of Lydia, who sold beautiful cloth. Like Lydia, as you learn more about Jesus your faith will grow.

Celebrating with Music
Teach the children the fourth verse of "Lord, I Want to Be a Christian" by playing a recording or singing.

More Exploring
Play the Bible Verse Echo Game, using the following Scripture verses.

To play, ask the children to listen carefully to the Bible verse. Then, when you say, "Do I hear an echo?" everyone, including you, will repeat the verse. You may want to break the verses into smaller phrases.

- "I have fought the good fight, finished the race, and kept the faith." (2 Timothy 4:7)

- "Don't be troubled. Trust in God. Trust also in me." (John 14:1)

- "Trust in the Lord with all your heart." (Proverbs 3:5)

- "Jesus responded to them, 'Have faith in God!'" (Mark 11:22)

Bonus Activity
Play "Duck, Duck, Goose," except say, "Red, Red, Purple."

The children sit in a circle. IT walks around the circle tapping each child on the head as they pass, saying "Red." Then, IT will tap a child and say, "Purple." Purple jumps up and chases IT around the outside of the circle back to Purple's seat. If Purple tags IT before IT sits down, IT goes to the center of the circle. Now Purple becomes the new IT. Continue as time permits or until there is only one child left in the circle.

Saying Goodbye
Give the children their Fancy Fabric Prints.

Say: Your prints are wonderful! When you see some beautiful cloth or the color purple this week, think of Lydia.

Supplies

- Purple construction paper or cardstock
- Paint color sample cards
- Scissors
- Glue

Note

If you have young children, cut the samples into geometric shapes (squares, triangles, rectangles) ahead of time.

Lord, I want to be like Jesus in my heart, in my heart.
Lord, I want to be like Jesus in my heart.
In my heart, in my heart.
Lord, I want to be like Jesus in my heart.

Supplies

- Box of crayons

Supplies

- Picture of a rainbow

Pray

Creator of Colors, thank you for the gift of colorful rainbows and your promise not to flood the whole earth again. When we see rainbows, God, we'll think of you. Amen.

Rainbow Covenant

Message:

Rainbows are a sign of God's promise.

Greeting with a Crayon Box

Greet the children. Hold up the crayon box. Pull out these colors in the order listed: red, orange, yellow, green, blue, purple.

Ask: Have you ever seen a rainbow in the sky or in a picture?

Say: Rainbows appear when light shines through raindrops, fog, or mist in a certain way. It's exciting to look at a rainbow, because we don't see them every time it rains. A rainbow always shows its colors in the same order *(Show the crayons again.)*: red at the top, orange, yellow, green, blue, and purple at the bottom.

Getting Set for the Story

Show a picture of a rainbow or color one on a piece of paper.

Say: God told Noah to build the ark, which is a very big boat, and to fill the boat with every animal, bird, and creeping thing living on the earth. Noah did as God asked. God explained that there would be rain for forty days and forty nights, making a great flood of water over the earth. So Noah, his family, and all the creatures were safe on the ark during the rain and flood.

Telling the Story

After forty days and forty nights of pouring rain, Noah opened a window on the ark to peek outside. The rain had stopped. Noah brought a raven to the window to see if the bird could find dry land anywhere. The raven flew out and back, so Noah sent a dove out too. The dove came back soon because there was no dry land or tree branch to sit on.

Seven days later, Noah sent the dove out again. This time the dove came back with a twig of fresh olive leaves. The flood waters were going away!

After seven more days, Noah sent the dove out, and the dove didn't return. Noah was glad! The ground must be drying. Noah took the roof covering off the ark. He could see for himself that the flood waters were gone and the ground was really drying out.

God spoke to Noah, saying all the people and animals could leave to live on dry land again.

Then God decided there would never again be a flood over all the earth.

God said, "I am making a promise to you, a covenant to you, that I will never again flood the earth. I make this covenant with you and your children and your children's children, as well as the living creatures."

A rainbow spread across the sky and God said, "I have placed a bow in the clouds; it will be a symbol of the covenant between me and the earth."

So Noah looked up at the beautiful rainbow. God said, "When I see the bow in the clouds, I will remember my covenant with you."

Exploring

Make Rainbow Fuzzy Wuzzies in celebration of God's gift of color.

You will need multi-colored yarn, available in craft stores or craft departments where yarn is sold. It's best to wrap the skein of yarn into smaller balls.

Precut 18-inch lengths of yarn to tie the Fuzzie Wuzzies, one piece of yarn per child.

Say: The rainbow brought Noah comfort. He knew that after the flood, God promised there would be no more floods to destroy the whole earth. Let's make fun Rainbow Fuzzy Wuzzies to help remember God's promise.

Demonstrate how to wrap the yarn around the width of an index card about thirty times. On one side of the card, slip an 18-inch length of yarn around the wrapped yarn. Knot tightly. Turn the card over and cut through all of the looped yarn. Slip from the card.

Have the children wrap the yarn and then slip through the 18-inch tie. Help them knot the yarn. Cutting through the wrapped yarn can be difficult. It's best to do this for younger children.

Celebrating with Music

Teach the children "If You're Happy and You Know It" with some new words. Each child will need crayons in the rainbow colors.

Sing about each rainbow color: red, orange, yellow, green, blue, and purple. If you don't have a complete set of rainbow colors for each child, they can hold up just one or two colors.

More Exploring

Say: We've got plenty of colors right here in Children's Church! Let's do some counting.

Ask the children to raise their hands if they are wearing the color: red, orange, yellow, green, blue, purple, white, black, brown, pink, and tan.

Count the number each time. When you are finished, tally up the votes and announce the Third Place, Second Place, and First Place Color Winners.

Say: Color makes our world brighter, happier, and more beautiful. The colors we see in nature have encouraged people to create paints, dyes, stains, inks, and even crayons, so that we can add even more color to our lives.

Bonus Activity

Search for "Rainbow Coloring Page" on the internet to find fun pages to print off for the children, or let them draw a rainbow free-hand.

Saying Goodbye

Hand out the Rainbow Fuzzie Wuzzies.

Say: God has blessed us with joyful colors. Let's shake our Fuzzy Wuzzies with happy thanks!

Supplies

- Multi-colored yarn
- Index cards
- Scissors

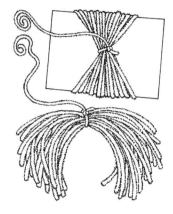

If you're happy and you know it, hold up red.
If you're happy and you know it, hold up red.
If you're happy and you know it, then let your rainbow show it;
If you're happy and you know it, hold up red.

[Repeat with other colors as desired.]

Supplies

- Paper
- Pencil

Supplies

- Coloring page from internet or drawing paper
- Crayons

Worship Spirit

Bible Verse
I rejoiced with those who said to me, "Let's go to the LORD's house!" (Psalm 122:1)

Supplies
- Hymnal
- Paper and crayons or photo of your church building

Come to Worship

Message:
The worship service is a time to worship God.

Greeting with a Hymnal
Draw a simple drawing or obtain a photograph of your church. Tuck it into a hymnal with one end poking out.

Greet the children. Hold up the hymnal. Choose a child to come forward and pull out the picture. Have the child show the picture to the group.

Ask: What's this? Why do you think people sometimes call a church "God's house?"

Say: Listen to a Bible verse about coming to God's house.

Read the Bible verse, and then have the children say it with you. Encourage them to say it one more time in their happiest voices.

Ask: When you come to the worship service, what do you see? What do you hear? What do you do? Do you like to come to worship?

Say: The worship service is a time to worship God. We're happy to come to worship to praise God, to sing hymns and hear the organ and choir, to listen to the Bible and words from our pastor, and to be with one another.

Getting Set for the Story
Hold up your hands and wiggle your fingers.

Say: We're going to pretend today that our fingers are people coming to church to worship God. Let's all hold up our Worship People.

Teach children the words and motions to "Here Is the Church."

Here is the church, (Fold hands with fingers inside.)

And here is the steeple. (Bring index fingers up to touch at tips.)

Open the doors (Move thumbs apart.)

And see all the people. (Turn hands over and wiggle fingers.)

Depending on how worship is conducted at your church, you may want to make some changes in the story. Before Children's Church, practice the finger motions so you are familiar with them.

Telling the Story

Now let's use those Worship People to pretend they are happily coming to church. Then we'll show them worshiping God and greeting one another. Here we go!

Make your Worship People walk up the sidewalk. Let them smile and wave to people as they go. *(Make fingers walk and then turn them up to wave to people.)*

Now the Worship People are walking into the church. They shake hands with one of the greeters. *(Have a finger on one hand bend toward a finger on the other.)* Next they take a bulletin and walk to their seats. *(Walk fingers and then put them upright.)* They choose a pew *(or chair)* and sit down. *(Bend fingers as if sitting down.)*

The organ starts up! The Worship People look to see the choir and pastor coming in. Now the Worship People stand for the opening hymn. *(Stand fingers straight.)* The Worship People start to sing. *(Sway fingers back and forth.)*

During the service, the Worship People sit and stand *(Have fingers go straight up and bend several times.)*, the Worship People pray *(Bend fingers downward.)*, and they listen to announcements and prayer concerns, Bible readings, and the pastor's sermon. *(Bend fingers as if sitting.)* When the pastor makes a joke, they laugh. *(Wiggle fingers as if laughing.)* They listen carefully, too, to the pastor's words about God, Jesus, and how we should live as Christians. *(Keep fingers steady.)*

At the end of the worship service, the Worship People stand for a final hymn. *(Hold fingers straight up.)* They stand still while the pastor says the final prayer and the choir sings a closing song.

The service is over. The Worship People leave their pews *(or seats)* and move about. They greet one another with handshakes *(Have a finger on one hand bend toward a finger on the other.)* or hugs. *(Wrap a finger on one hand around a finger on the other.)* They exchange happy words of greeting *(Have fingers on one hand wiggle toward fingers on the other.)* and they shake hands with the pastor as they leave the service. *(Have a finger on one hand bend toward a finger on the other.)*

As the Worship People walk down the sidewalk, they continue chatting with each other. *(Bend fingers of one hand toward fingers of the other.)* They are happy they went to the Lord's house, their church, to worship God.

Exploring

Children will make Open Door Churches filled with worshipers!

For the inside of the church, you'll need light-colored construction paper. The doors and the roof can be made out of light or darker colors. Consider using different colors for the doors and roof.

Cut and assemble the churches ahead of time. To make the church doors, fold a sheet of paper in half. Cut along the fold. Fold again and cut along the fold. This makes two sets of doors. Place a set of doors at the bottom of a sheet of paper. Tape or staple each door to the outside edge.

Pray

God of Our Faith, we thank you for our church, whose people gather together to praise and worship you. Help us to continue to be happy worshipers throughout our lives. Amen.

Supplies

- Construction paper
- Scissors
- Crayons
- Tape or stapler

Our church is [name of church], our church is [name of church].
Alleluia, Alleluia!
Our church is [name of church].

Our church is on [location, such as "on the corner," "on a hill," or the street name].

Our church is made of [brick, stone, wood, and so forth].

Our pastor's name is [name of pastor].

[If you have more than one pastor, sing a verse for each one.]

Supplies
- Graham crackers
- Frosting in a tube
- Napkins

Supplies
- Long sheet of paper
- Crayons or markers
- Tape or stapler

For the roofs, fold a sheet of paper in half. Fold in half again. Cut diagonally from the unfolded corner to the opposite corner to make a triangular roof. Open. This yields four roofs. Staple or tape a roof above the door on the churches.

Give each child an Open Door Church.

Say: Our church opens our doors wide. Everyone is welcome to worship with us!

Have the children draw happy worshipers inside the church and then decorate the outside. Invite them to pass the churches around so that everyone can open the doors and peek inside.

Celebrating with Music
The song "Our Church" is set to the tune of "The Farmer in the Dell."

Say: Today, we're going to sing a song about our church, and we're going to make up some of the verses ourselves! Ready?

Sing any other verses that you or the children come up with, and then finish with a final verse.

Sing: We're glad to come to church. . . .

More Exploring
Children will love creating a delicious Graham Cracker Church. You'll need one or several tubes of frosting and graham crackers.

Give each child one whole graham cracker. Use the frosting to draw the church shape. Show the children how to squeeze a frosting rectangle on the bottom half of the cracker. This is the church building. Then show them how to add a frosting triangle for the church roof. Finish with a cross on top of the roof.

If you have leftover graham crackers and frosting, let the children make more Graham Cracker Churches to share with others.

Bonus Activity
Make a festive paper banner to welcome worshipers to church. Write the Bible verse at the top. Have the children decorate the banner with crosses, churches, or happy faces and then sign their names. Hang the welcome banner on a wall or railing, on the church door, or in the narthex.

Saying Goodbye
Give children their Open Door Churches.

Say: The worship service is a time to worship God. We're glad we can come to the Lord's house!

Praying in Worship

Message:
We pray in church.

Greeting with a Hymnal
Write the word "AMEN" on the paper in bold letters. Fold the paper and tuck it into the hymnal with one end poking out.

Greet the children. Hold up the hymnal. Choose a child to come forward and pull out the paper. Have the child show the word.

Say: When we pray, we end our prayers by saying, "Amen." The word "amen" comes from the Hebrew word "aman," which means "firm" or "sure." When we say "Amen," we are stating that we are sure that God is listening to our prayer.

Say: You can pray anytime and anywhere. You can pray in bed at night, at the dinner table, while you're in school, or when you're playing outside. Every week during our worship service, we pray. Today, we're going to talk about the prayers we pray when we worship God at church.

Getting Set for the Story
The story focuses on prayers in the worship service. Be sure to include any other types of prayers used in your church not mentioned in the story. Consider bringing in bulletins for the children and showing them any prayers printed there.

During the story, you will lead the children in praying the Lord's Prayer. If your congregation uses a different version of the prayer, you may want to teach the children that version.

Telling the Story
In Old Testament times, people gathered in the Temple to pray. In the New Testament, we read of Jesus praying by himself and with his disciples. One day, he said to his disciples, "When you pray, pray like this." Then he taught them a prayer that we pray every week in our worship service. We call it "The Lord's Prayer." Let's pray it together. Close your eyes, and after I say a line, we'll say that line together:

Our Father in heaven, *(repeat)*

Hallowed be your name, *(repeat)*

your kingdom come, *(repeat)*

your will be done, *(repeat)*

on earth as in heaven. *(repeat)*

Give us today our daily bread. *(repeat)*

Forgive us our sins *(repeat)*

As we forgive those who sin against us. *(repeat)*

Save us from the trial, *(repeat)*

And deliver us from evil. *(repeat)*

Supplies
- Hymnal
- Paper
- Crayon or marker

Supplies
- Church bulletins or orders of service (optional)

Pray

God of Our Faith, we're glad we can gather together to worship you.
Response: Thanks be to God.

We're glad you created a beautiful world.
Response: Thanks be to God.

We're glad for our church and the people who worship here.
Response: Thanks be to God.

And we're glad you hear our prayers.
Response: Thanks be to God.

And let all the people say, "Amen."
Response: Amen.

Supplies

- Paper
- Pen or pencil
- Index cards, tape, and yarn or ribbon (optional)

Praise God, from whom all blessings flow;
Praise God, all creatures here below;
Praise God above, ye heavenly host;
Praise Father, Son, and Holy Ghost.

For the kingdom, the power, and the glory are yours *(repeat)*

Now and forever. Amen. *(repeat)*

(You may want to say the prayer with the children a second time.)

After Jesus went to heaven, the early Christians gathered together.

(Read the Bible verse.)

Prayer was important during these early church services, and it's important today. We pray prayers of praise during our worship service, honoring God and thanking God for all our blessings. We pray prayers of confession, telling God our sins and asking for forgiveness. We pray before we read from the Bible, asking God to help us understand the words and message of the Bible. We pray after the offering, thanking God for the gifts of money and asking God to help us use the money wisely. During our worship service, we pray silently too. Let's close our eyes, bow our heads, and say a silent prayer to God. *(Pause for silent prayer.)*

A litany is a type of prayer. The pastor or leader says a line, and the congregation responds. Today, I'm the leader. After each line of the prayer, you will respond with the words, "Thanks be to God."

(Lead the children in practicing the response. Tell them that at the end of the prayer, you will say, "Amen," and they will respond with "Amen.")

Exploring

The children will work with you to compose a Prayer of Thanksgiving. Check with your pastor to see if he or she is willing to incorporate the prayer in an upcoming service. If so, be sure to tell the children they are writing a prayer to be used in the worship service.

Say: In worship, our prayers offer thanks and praise God for our many blessings. Today, let's take turns saying things we are thankful for. I'll write them down, and then we'll pray them as a Prayer of Thanksgiving.

If you want this activity to take longer, you can ask the children to name things by category: a person they are thankful for, an animal, a place, a food, an activity.

When the list is complete, ask the children to bow their heads for prayer.

Pray: Holy God, you have given us many blessings. Thank you for all of these things: *(Slowly read the list.)* Amen.

Give the list to your pastor if he or she has agreed to use it in an upcoming worship service. (You may want to do a bit of editing.)

Consider writing the children's responses on separate index cards and attaching the cards to a long length of yarn or ribbon. The garland can be used to decorate a bulletin board or wall at church, with a sign next to it saying, "Thank you, God, for these blessings."

Celebrating with Music

Teach children "Praise God, from Whom All Blessings Flow" by playing a recording or singing the song for them. If your church uses a different prayer response song, you will want to teach that one.

Say: During worship, we sometimes sing prayers. The song we're going to sing today, "Praise God, from Whom All Blessings Flow," is also called the "Doxology." A "doxology" is a short prayer of praise.

More Exploring

Decorate Prayer Pockets to teach children about congregational prayer concerns.

You will need the names of two or more members of your congregation who are on the church prayer list due to illness, bereavement, or another difficulty. Write these names on separate slips of paper for each child. If you have a church directory with pictures, bring in the directory to show the children. This will help them connect names with faces. If prayer concerns are printed in the bulletin or the church newsletter, you may want to show this to the children.

Say: Every week during our worship service, we pray for people who are sick, grieving, or suffering from another difficulty.

Read the names of the people you recorded on the slips of paper. Say a word about each one. If you have a pictorial directory, show the children the person's photo.

Say: Let's make Prayer Pockets! We'll slip the names of the people in the pockets. At home, you can take out the slips from time to time to help you remember to pray for those people. You can add other names, too.

Have each child write "AMEN" on a coffee filter and then decorate around the letters. When the Prayer Pockets are finished, hand out the slips of paper. Have the children tuck the slips inside.

Bonus Activity

On the internet, search for "Lord's Prayer coloring pages" for the children to color. Consider gluing the decorated pages to folders to use to store school papers, birthday cards, and other paper mementos.

Saying Goodbye

Make sure children take their Prayer Pockets and coloring pages with them.

Say: At the end of the service, the pastor prays a final prayer called a benediction. The congregation stands up for this prayer. Let's stand up. I'll say a line of the benediction and then you say it back. Ready:

Go forth in peace. *(repeat)*

The grace of the Lord Jesus Christ *(repeat)*

and the love of God *(repeat)*

and the communion of the Holy Spirit *(repeat)*

be with you all. *(repeat)*

Now let's all say together the word we say at the end of our prayers: AMEN!

Say: We're glad we can pray special prayers to God during our worship service. Remember, though, that any time is a good time to pray to God.

Supplies

- #4 cone coffee filters
- Crayons
- Small slips of paper
- Marker
- Photo directory of your church (optional)
- Current church bulletin or newsletter (optional)

Supplies

- Lord's Prayer coloring pages
- Crayons
- Manila folders and glue (optional)

Speak to each other with psalms, hymns, and spiritual songs; sing and make music to the Lord in your hearts. (Ephesians 5:19)

Supplies

- Hymnal
- Paper
- Crayon or marker

Make Music to the Lord

Message:

Music is an important part of Christian worship.

Greeting with a Hymnal

Draw a simple face with an open mouth to represent someone singing. Fold the paper and tuck it into a hymnal.

Greet the children. Hold up the hymnal. Choose a child to come forward and pull out the picture. Have the child show the picture.

Ask: What is the person doing in this picture?

Say: We sing praises to God during our worship service and we hear special songs the choir sings. We also hear instrumental music, which is music without any singing at all.

Read the Bible verse.

Say: In Old Testament times, people worshiped God with singing and with instrumental music. When the Christian Church was formed, the early Christians used music too. Today, at our church, music is an important part of our worship service.

Getting Set for the Story

Today's story celebrates music in worship. When you introduce each word, you will lead the children in singing a verse using the word.

Telling the Story

Today, we're going to study words that relate to music in Christian worship. I'll introduce each word. Then we'll sing a song about that word before we talk about it some more. We'll sing each verse to the tune of "Row, Row, Row Your Boat." Ready?

HYMNS

Sing: We sing hymns in church as we worship God. *(repeat)*

Say: Hymns are songs written to worship God and celebrate our faith.

Ask: What are some of your favorite hymns? Do you know what a book of hymns is called? *(hymnal)*

CHOIR

Sing: The choir sings for us, beautiful, beautiful songs.
    The choir sings for us as we worship God.

Say: A choir is a group of singers who practice and then use Christian music during the worship service. Do you know the name of someone who sings in our choir? Would you like to sing in the choir?

CHOIR DIRECTOR

Sing: The choir director chooses songs and leads the choir at church.
    The choir director leads the choir as we worship God.

Say: The choir director chooses the anthem and leads the choir during practice and during the worship service.

Ask: Who is our choir director? Would you like to be a choir director?

ORGANIST/PIANIST

Sing: The organist *(or pianist)* plays for us music on the organ *(or piano)*
    The organist *(or pianist)* plays for us as we worship God.

Say: The organist *(or pianist)* practices and then plays music during the worship service. In many churches, the organist *(or pianist)* is also the choir director.

Make up additional verses about other types of music used at your church.

Exploring

Musical Meditations connect music to spiritual thinking. Children will let the music inspire them as they create with their eyes closed.

Say: Christians use music to worship God. It helps us feel close to God.

Say: Today we're going to color Musical Meditations. Listen to the music as you think about God and what the music says to you. With your eyes closed, color. Let your hands move across the paper to the music.

When the music is finished, invite children to open their eyes. Ask the children one by one to tell how the music made them feel and show their pictures to the group.

If time permits, repeat this activity with eyes open, using the same song. Share the pictures once again.

Celebrating with Music

Put children into four groups.

Say: In worship, we sometimes hear other musical instruments besides the organ or piano. Today, let's pretend we've got flutes, trumpets, drums, and cymbals.

Assign children to the following instruments and the sounds they make: flute (dee, dee, dee), trumpet (toot-toot-toot), drums (boom, boom, boom), or cymbals (clang, clang, clang).

Say: You're a Bible Band! I'm going to sing the words to "Jesus Love Me," and you make the sound of your instrument to the tune.

More Exploring

Invite a guest musician to bring her or his musical instrument to Children's Church. Tell the musician you would like her or him to play Christian music for the children, but other selections are welcome too.

Bonus Activity

Tell the children that in Bible times, people often worshiped God with dance and tambourines. Have children color paper plates and then staple or tape crepe paper streamers, ribbon, or yarn to the edges of the plate. Play music and ask the children to dance and play their tambourines.

Saying Goodbye

Give children their Musical Meditations drawings and their tambourines.

Say: Music is one of God's great gifts to the world. We're glad that we can use the gift of music to worship and praise God.

Pray

God of Our Faith, we thank you for organs and pianos and trumpets and tambourines and flutes and drums and tubas and clarinets and guitars and all the musical instruments we can use to praise you with music. Most of all, we thank you for our singing voices. Amen.

Supplies

- Paper
- Crayons
- Recording of instrumental Christian Music
- Music player

Supplies

- Paper plates
- Crayons
- Crepe paper streamers, ribbon, or yarn
- Stapler or tape
- Recording of instrumental Christian Music
- Music player

Let your priests be dressed in righteousness; let your faithful shout for joy! (Psalm 132:9)

Supplies

- Hymnal
- Paper and crayons or photograph of your pastor

The Pastor

Message:

The pastor plans and leads the worship service.

Greeting with a Hymnal

Draw a simple picture of your pastor or locate a photograph of him or her. Tuck the picture into a hymnal.

If your church has more than one pastor, draw pictures of each one and refer to all the pastors when you speak about them.

Greet the children. Hold up the hymnal. Choose a child to come forward and pull out the picture. Have the child show the picture.

Say: This is a drawing of our pastor, *(name)*. He *(or she)* preaches; teaches; visits the sick and shut in; conducts weddings, funerals, baptisms, and confirmation; serves on church committees; and works in many other ways to help our congregation.

Getting Set for the Story

Not all pastors prepare for worship in the same way. If practical, you may want to chat with your pastor about how he or she prepares for the service so that you can share some specifics with the children.

Telling the Story

Let's pretend you're the pastor preparing for the worship service. I'll lead you in some actions as I tell the story. Ready, pastors?

First you're going to read the Bible verses set for Sunday. Take out your Bible and turn the pages. *(Pretend to turn pages.)* Ah. There are the verses. Read the verses. *(Move head back and forth.)*

Now think about the verses. *(Tap finger on head a few times.)* You'll use them to come up with a sermon to preach to your congregation. Keep thinking while you drive to visit someone who is sick. *(Pretend to drive.)* Keep thinking while you walk to the post office. *(Walk in place.)* Keep thinking while you water a plant at church that is looking droopy. *(Pretend to water plant.)*

Pray about those verses. Ask God to help you understand them. *(Press hands together in prayer.)*

Go to your bookshelves and pull down books about the Bible. *(Pretend to pull down books.)* Read passages from the books for ideas, information, and words you can quote in your sermon. *(Pretend to pick up a book, turn pages, and read—do this several times.)*

Now, start to write your sermon. *(Pretend to type on a keyboard.)* Think. *(Tap finger on head a few times.)* Write and write and write. *(Type.)* Then go back and fix up what you wrote. *(Type.)* Your sermon is almost finished. Phew! *(Swish hand across forehead.)*

You have more to do to get ready for worship. Plan the announcements, the prayers, the call to worship, the children's sermon, and other parts of the service. Talk with the choir director and others helping with the worship service. *(Pretend to talk on telephone.)*

And now it's Sunday morning! Before you leave for church, have a cup of coffee or tea and relax for a minute. *(Lift pretend mug to mouth and sip.)* It's going to be a busy morning, but you worked hard to get ready for worship and your congregation appreciates you!

Exploring

Make Fancy Page Markers for your pastor to use.

Before Children's Church, cut the index cards in half lengthwise.

Have the children decorate the page markers with Christian symbols such as the fish, cross, butterfly, angel, heart, rainbow, and dove. Have the children write their names on the markers. Collect the Fancy Page Markers for the pastor.

Celebrating with Music

Before Children's Church, ask your pastor what her or his favorite Christian songs were when she or he was a child.

Say: Our pastor loved this song when she *(or he)* was little. Let's sing it today in her *(or his)* honor.

Sing the song and any other songs the pastor mentioned.

More Exploring

Your pastor will appreciate Pastor Postcards that he or she can mail or bring to members of the congregation. If the Pastor Postcards are going to be mailed, use 4 x 6–inch index cards to meet postal requirements.

Children will decorate one side of the card with a drawing of a sheep. Have a simple sheep picture to show them. Draw a sheep (fluffy cloud, head, and four legs) or look for a cartoon image on the internet.

Set out supplies. Hold up the picture of the sheep.

Say: In the ancient language of Latin, "pastor" means "shepherd." Just as a shepherd leads sheep, a pastor leads a congregation.

Have the children decorate the index cards with drawings of a sheep. If the cards are lined, ask them to color the sheep on the unlined side.

Bonus Activity

Before Children's Church, ask your pastor to answer these questions, so you can share the answers with the children:

Why did you decide to become a pastor?

What was your best subject in school?

What is your favorite color? Your favorite flavor of ice cream? Your favorite book? Your favorite sport? Your favorite animal? Your favorite flower? Your favorite way to spend a vacation?

Saying Goodbye

Say: We're glad we have our pastor, *(name)*, to lead our congregation.

If practical, let the children help you deliver the Fancy Page Markers and the Pastor Postcards to your pastor. If not, tell the children you will deliver them soon.

Pray

God of Our Faith, thank you for our pastor(s), [name(s)]. Help [him/her/them] to lead our congregation. Amen.

Supplies

- Index cards
- Crayons
- Scissors

Supplies

- 4 x 6 index cards
- Markers
- Simple picture of a sheep

Bible Verse
He also saw a poor widow throw in two small copper coins worth a penny. (Luke 21:2)

Supplies
- Hymnal
- Coins

Supplies
- Pennies
- Offering container

Pray
God of Our Faith, thank you for the widow so long ago who gave all she had, two copper coins. Help us to be generous givers, too. Amen.

Supplies
- Copy paper
- Coins
- Crayons (unwrapped)
- Construction paper
- Stapler, glue or tape
- Offering container

Our Offering

Message:
The church uses the offering to do God's work.

Greeting with a Hymnal
Tuck four or more coins inside a hymnal.

Greet the children. Hold up the hymnal, taking care not to let the coins fall out. Choose a child to come forward.

Say: I've tucked something into this hymnal. I'd like you to shake it gently and see if it will tumble out.

When the coins fall out, ask the children to pick them up.

Say: We collect coins, dollars, and checks each week at church. This is called the offering.

Say: Our church needs money to pay our pastor and other staff members; to take care of our building; to pay our water and power bills; to pay for supplies for Sunday school crafts and choir music; and to help others in our community and around the world. That's why we collect an offering.

Getting Set for the Story
Give each child two pennies.

Ask: Did I just give you a lot of money?

Say: Two pennies is not a lot of money. In today's story, a woman is so poor that she only has two pennies to put into the offering plate. Let's see what happens. Hold tight to your pennies while I tell the story.

Telling the Story
One day, Jesus was at the Temple with his disciples. He watched rich people throwing their money into the collection box. Then Jesus saw a poor widow put two small copper coins worth a penny into the collection box.

He said, "I promise you that this poor widow has put in more than all the other people. They were giving money they had left over. The widow is hopelessly poor. Even though she is so poor, she has given all that she has."

Jesus used the story of the widow and her two coins to help the disciples understand that God wants us to be generous when we give our offering to the church. God doesn't really want us to give up everything we have, but Jesus wants us to understand the importance of giving generously.

You're each going to get a turn pretending you are the poor widow. You'll come forward and put your two pennies into the collection box. As you do, think about the widow so long ago and the generosity she showed.

Exploring
Children will create Coin Rubbing Reminders.

Copy paper works well for coin rubbing; heavier paper will not. Bring in pennies, nickels, dimes, and quarters, one of each type of coin for each child. If this isn't practical, simply bring in four or more coins per child.

Talk with the children about the offering at your church. Explain how the offering is collected during the worship service and include a few words about any special offerings or collections at your church. If you collect an offering during Sunday school, discuss that with the children, too.

Say: Let's make a Coin Rubbing Reminder for you to put on your refrigerator or hang in your room at home. When you see it, you'll remember to get some coins ready to bring to church each Sunday.

Show the children how to slip the coins under the paper and then glide the crayon gently over the surface until the impression appears. When they are finished making coin rubbings, have them write their names on their picture and a reminder such as "Don't Forget!" Mount each picture to a sheet of construction paper using a stapler, glue, or tape.

Collect the coins in an offering container.

Celebrating with Music
Teach children the refrain "Jesu, Jesu" by playing a recording or singing the song for them. Explain that "Jesu" means "Jesus."

More Exploring
Play Bible Verse Roundabout. Have the children form a circle.

Supplies
• Ball

Say: Listen to this Bible verse that talks about giving: "God loves a cheerful giver" (2 Corinthians 9:7).

Ask the children to repeat the verse with you: "God loves a cheerful giver."

Say: Now let's play Bible Verse Roundabout!

Explain that you are going to start a ball around the circle. The first person will say the first word of the verse, "God," and pass the ball to the person on his or her right. That person will say the next word, "loves." This will continue until the verse is said as the ball moves around the circle. When the verse is finished, the next person will begin the verse again.

As children get the hang of the game, speed things up. You can also call for them to reverse directions.

Here are three more verses about giving you can use for more rounds:

"Feed my sheep." (John 21:17)

"It is more blessed to give than to receive." (Acts 20:35)

"Give, and it will be given to you." (Luke 6:38)

Bonus Activity
Send the children on a Cookie Coin Hunt. Before Children's Church, cut foil into small squares and use the squares to cover round cookies. Hide the Cookie Coins. Announce, "We're going on a coin hunt!" Let the children have the fun of hunting for the coins and then enjoying them for a snack.

Supplies
• Round cookies
• Aluminum foil
• Scissors

Saying Goodbye
Give the children their Coin Rubbing Reminders.

Say: Just like the widow was generous with her offering, God wants us to be generous in our offerings. The church uses the offering to do God's work.

God's word continued to grow and increase.
(Acts 12:24)

Supplies

- Hymnal
- Bible
- Paper
- Crayon
- Pen or marker

Supplies

- Bibles

Pray

I will give thanks to you, my Lord, among all the peoples; I will make music to you among the nations because your faithful love is as high as heaven; your faithfulness reaches the clouds.
(Psalm 57:9-10) Amen.

God's Word

Message:

Our worship is centered on the teachings of the Bible.

Greeting with a Hymnal

Draw a simple outline of an open book. Write the Bible verse inside the outline. Fold the drawing and place it in a hymnal.

Greet the children. Hold up the hymnal. Choose a child to come forward and pull out the picture. Have the child show the picture to the group.

Say: This is a Bible and a verse from the Bible.

Invite a reader to read the verse or read the verse yourself. Then lead the children in saying the verse. Hold up a real Bible.

Ask: Does this verse mean that the words of the Bible keep getting bigger?

Say: No, the words themselves don't really get bigger. The verse means that the early Christians told others about Jesus. More and more people understood the word of God and became Christians. In this way, the word of God grew and increased.

Getting Set for the Story

If your church has Bibles available for use, bring them in for the children. Even a child who doesn't read yet will appreciate the opportunity to hold the Bible and look through it.

Telling the Story

Hold up the Bible.

Say: The Bible is the book of our faith. It's divided into the Old Testament and the New Testament. The Old Testament covers the time period before the birth of Jesus. The New Testament is the story of Jesus and the early church. Both the Old Testament and the New Testament are divided into sections called "books." There are sixty-six books in the Bible.

Show the children where the Old and New Testaments are located. Point out some of the books of the Bible.

Say: The Bible is filled with history, law, poetry, letters, and stories. Kids especially like the stories! One favorite is Noah and the Ark. Noah's story is close to the beginning of the Bible, in the very first book, Genesis.

Open the Bible and show children Genesis 7:6-12.

Ask: Let's see if you know this story! What did God tell Noah to build? What did Noah take on the ark? How long did it rain?

Say: At the end of the story, God makes a promise with a rainbow. Let's read that passage. *(Read Genesis 9:13.)*

Say: The New Testament has stories too! Another favorite is the Christmas story. Let's read some of that important story. *(Read Luke 2:8-16.)*

Say: Christians all over the world listen to the words of the Bible as they are read during the worship service. Christian worship is centered on the teachings of the Bible.

Exploring

Bible Mobiles help children remember how to spell the important book of our faith, the B-I-B-L-E!

Each mobile takes two straws and five index cards. It also takes five pieces of yarn in varying lengths from eight to eighteen inches. Cut the yarn ahead of time, keeping the sizes separate. You'll also need a yarn hanger about eighteen inches long for each mobile.

Have the children write the letters B-I-B-L-E on five cards, one letter per card, on both sides. If you have children who do not write yet, prepare the cards ahead of time. Let the children decorate the cards any way they like.

Place one straw on top of the other to form a cross. Tape the straws together at the center. To make the mobile secure, tape in both directions.

Have the children tape each decorated index card to a piece of yarn. Help them tape the yarn onto the crossed straws. (Tape four of the cards at the ends of the extensions of the cross, and the fifth one in the very center of the cross. In this way the strings won't tangle.)

Give each child a yarn hanger. Use a knot to tie the hanger to the mobile at the center of the crossed straws.

Celebrating with Music

Teach children "The B-I-B-L-E" by playing a recording or singing the song for them.

More Exploring

Let the children watch you roll a sheet of paper into a scroll. Secure the scroll with yarn or ribbon.

Say: In Bible times, books looked very different than our books do today. Books in Bible times were written on long pieces of paper and rolled into a scroll. To read the book, you unrolled it! Let's play "Who's Got the Scroll?"

Pick one child to be the Scroll Guesser. Have the rest of the children form a tight circle around the Scroll Guesser. Tell them they will hand the scroll, behind their backs, around the circle. As they do, they will chant, "Scroll, scroll, who's got the scroll?" They should make their arms move as little as possible while passing the scroll. After a short time, call, "STOP!" The Scroll Guesser must guess who has the scroll. Play until everyone gets a turn as Scroll Guesser and as time permits.

Bonus Activity

Help children learn Bible verses! Divide the children into two groups. Place the groups as far away from each other as possible. Teach the children a Bible verse. Assign one half of the verse to one group and one half to the other group. Have them say the verse back and forth. To add to the fun, let them sing the verse, shout the verse, whisper the verse, say the verse quickly, say it slowly, and twirl around as they call out the verse.

Saying Goodbye

Give the children their Bible Mobiles.

Say: Our Christian worship is centered on the teachings of the Bible. We thank God for giving us the Bible, the guidebook for our Christian faith.

Supplies
- Drinking straws
- Index cards
- Crayons
- Yarn
- Scissors
- Tape

The B-I-B-L-E, yes, that's the book for me!
I stand alone on the Word of God, the B-I-B-L-E!

Supplies
- Paper
- Yarn or ribbon

Bible Verses

I rejoiced with those who said to me/"Let's go to the LORD's house!" (Psalm 122:1)

I keep your word close, in my heart,/so that I won't sin against you. (Psalm 119:11)

In the beginning was the Word/and the Word was with God and the Word was God. (John 1:1)

The grass dries up; the flower withers,/but our God's word will exist forever. (Isaiah 40:8)

Fall Faith

Bible Verse

Turn your ear and hear the words of the wise; focus your mind on my knowledge. (Proverbs 22:17)

Supplies

- New pencils
- Basket
- Cloth

School!

Message:

We learn at school and church.

Greeting with a Basket

Surprise the children with brand new pencils. If this isn't practical, simply put two or three pencils in the basket. Cover them with a cloth.

Greet the children. Hold up the basket. Ask a child to remove the cloth and hold up the pencils.

Ask: What are these? What do you do with them? Do kids use these in school?

Say: Kids use pencils in school for math, to write compositions and stories, to take notes, and to answer questions on tests. We go to school to learn, and we come to Sunday school and Children's Church to learn too.

Read the Bible verse from Proverbs.

Say: These words were spoken by a teacher in the Bible. Learning is important. God wants us to be good learners.

If you have new pencils to give the children, hand them out now or explain that they will receive a gift of brand-new pencils at the end of Children's Church.

Getting Set for the Story

Let each child say the name of their daycare, preschool, or elementary school or tell the group if they are homeschooled. If you have younger children who don't fit into any of these categories, remind them that they will go to school before too long.

Ask: We learn at Sunday school and Children's Church too! Can you tell me something you've learned in Sunday school or Children's Church?

You may need to urge children on with some more directed questions.

Say: Hooray for school and everything we learn!

Say: Middle schools and high schools have cheerleaders who cheer for the school's teams. For today's story, you're going to be cheerleaders cheering for learning and for schools everywhere.

Say: We learn to spell at school. Let's all practice spelling "school."

Lead the children in slowly spelling out the letters of "school."

Say: Good job! In our story, every time you hear the word "school," we'll do this cheer: S-C-H-O-O-L spells "school"!

Practice this a few times and then begin the story.

Telling the Story

Here's something that's really cool,

Kids learn important things at SCHOOL!

They learn to spell and they learn to read,

At SCHOOL they learn about stars and seeds.

They study history and they study math,

At SCHOOL they even play and laugh.

Sunday SCHOOL and Children's Church, too,

Are taught especially for kids like you.

Here we learn about our Christian faith,

And leave this SCHOOL with a smiling face.

For SCHOOL during the week and our SCHOOL here,

Let's give a final loud happy cheer!

(You may want to read the story again, asking children to just listen this time.)

Exploring

Signature Folders are just right for storing school papers!

Children will sign their names to each folder. Markers are best for this, but crayons will work if need be.

Say: School kids have lots of papers! Let's make folders for you to store your papers in. We'll sign each other's folders, so we can be reminded of one another when we're at home.

Give each child a folder. Pick one up for yourself. Set out the markers. Have the children sign every folder. Sign them yourself, too. Encourage the children to add simple decorations next to their signatures such as a happy face or a butterfly.

Consider making a few extra folders to surprise your pastor, church secretary, and/or choir director. Parents and older siblings would appreciate a folder too.

Celebrating with Music

Sing the ABC's and "The B-I-B-L-E" to celebrate learning at school and at church. Next, let the children take turns suggesting favorite songs they sing in school and church.

Pray

God of Our Year, we think it's cool that we go to school! Help us to be good listeners and good learners. Amen.

Supplies
- Manila folders
- Markers or crayons

The B-I-B-L-E, yes, that's the book for me!
I stand alone on the Word of God, the B-I-B-L-E!

Supplies

- Twinkies®
- Life Savers® candies
- Yellow frosting
- Knife
- Plates
- Napkins
- Spoons
- Juice or water
- Cups

Supplies

- Apples
- Apple-themed books and resources

More Exploring

Celebrate back to school by making Twinkies® School Buses! Frosting that comes in tubes is the most convenient, but canned frosting or homemade will work too. White frosting can be colored yellow with food coloring.

Say: Some children walk to school. Some ride their bikes. Others ride to school in cars. Some go on subways or trains or even ferry boats. But lots of kids travel to school in yellow school buses! No matter how you get to school, it's important to be there because we go to school to learn.

Cut a rectangle from one end of each Twinkie® and lay it down to form the hood of the bus. The rounded top end should be away from the rest of the Twinkie® and the bottom should be touching the Twinkie®. The cut side will be touching the plate. Give a Twinkie® bus to each child.

Next, squirt a border of frosting around the top of the Twinkie® or spoon some frosting on the top. Show the children how to smooth the frosting down the sides with their spoon to create a yellow school bus. Add more frosting as needed.

Give each child four Life Savers®. Show them how to put the Life Savers® on either side of the bus. These are the wheels.

Lead everyone in a round of "The Wheels of the Bus." Then invite the children to eat their Twinkies® School Buses. Serve juice or water.

Bonus Activity

Since apples are a symbol of school and teachers, hold an Apple Festival! Show children the cover of *Around the Year in Children's Church*, share books and other resources about apples, and offer children an apple-tasting featuring a variety of apples. Conclude the festival by singing or saying the poem that honors the great apple man himself, Johnny Appleseed:

> Oh the Lord is good to me,
> and so I thank the Lord,
> for giving me the things I need,
> the sun, and the rain, and the apple seed.
> The Lord is good to me.

Saying Goodbye

Give the children their Signature Folders.

Say: Goodbye, good learners!

The Festival of the Booths

Message:
We learn about Old Testament traditions.

Greeting with a Basket
Place a small branch with leaves in the basket. Cover it with a cloth.

Greet the children. Hold up the basket. Ask a child to remove the cloth and hold up the branch.

Say: Today, we're going to talk about an Old Testament holiday that features branches. This holiday takes place in late September or early October. Let's find out more!

Getting Set for the Story
Ask: Have you ever slept outdoors in a tent or a hut? What did you hear and see and smell?

Say: Sleeping outdoors can be really fun. Today's story is about sleeping outdoors during a festival that began in the days of the Old Testament.

Telling the Story
In the Old Testament, the Jewish people lived in the wilderness for forty years while they were waiting for God to bring them into the Holy Land. Forty years is a long time! During that time, they didn't have regular houses. They slept in tents or other temporary shelters. To honor those years, after they were settled in the Holy Land, God commanded them to hold a festival called the "Festival of Booths." "Booths" was another word for the temporary homes they lived in. Some translations of the Bible call these homes "huts." Listen to God's instructions about the festival.

(Read Leviticus 23:39-43.)

Right after the fall crops were brought in, God said the people were to live in these booths or huts for seven days. And so the people did as God told them.

Today, Jewish families and some Christian families, too, keep this festival in the early fall. They set up temporary booths or huts. In Hebrew the word for these is "sukkot." Kids and grownups decorate the booths with branches, leaves, ornaments, and other decorations. They go inside the booths and have delicious fruit and other snacks. Sometimes they even sleep there all night long! This holiday, called "The Festival of the Booths," "Sukkot," or "Succoth," is a happy time that celebrates God's gift of the Holy Land and God's gift of a good harvest.

Exploring
Children will build and decorate a sukkah made of cards.

Make a sample to show them. For each sukkah, you will need three index cards. Cut one of the cards in half. Tape one half to each end of an index card; be sure the top and bottom are even. Fold the sides in at ninety-degree angles and stand the cards on edge. You've made the back and the sides of the sukkah. Another index card rested on the top is the roof.

Bible Verse
For seven days you must live in huts. Every citizen of Israel must live in huts.
(Leviticus 23:42)

Supplies
- Branch
- Basket
- Cloth

Pray
God of Our Year, we're glad for the delicious fruits and vegetables of the harvest. We're glad, too, that you led the Jewish people into the Holy Land. Thank you for guiding people years ago and for guiding and loving us now. Amen.

Note
"Sukkot" is the plural form of "sukkah." A sukkah is one booth.

Supplies
- Index cards
- Tape
- Scissors
- Crayons or markers

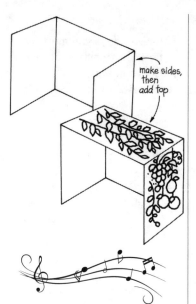

make sides, then add top

Come, ye thankful people, come,
Raise the song of harvest home.
All is safely gathered in
Ere the winter storms begin.
God our Maker doth provide
For our wants to be supplied.
Come to God's own temple, come,
Raise the song of harvest home.

Supplies
- Green leaves
- Copy paper
- Crayons (unwrapped)

Supplies
- Appliance box or table with sheet
- Apple slices or other fruit snack

Precut the side cards for the children.

Say: This is a sukkah made of cards. A real sukkah usually has leaves and branches on the roof, so color those on the roof of your card sukkah. And a real sukkah is often decorated with hanging fruit, so decorate the sides of your sukkah with fruit.

When they are finished, have the children set up their sukkot made of cards. Ask them to pretend their fingers are people. Let them walk their fingers and visit one another's sukkot.

Say: You can fold your sukkah up now. When you get home, set it up in your room to remember the Festival of the Booths. You might have some small dolls, toy animals, or figures that will enjoy checking it out!

Celebrating with Music
Say: The Festival of the Booths celebrated the harvest of crops much as Thanksgiving does. Let's sing a harvest hymn.

Teach children "Come, Ye Thankful People, Come" by playing a recording or singing the song for them.

More Exploring
Collect several varieties of green leaves if possible. If the leaves are gathered more than a few hours before Children's Church, it's best to press them between newspaper or paper towels with the help of heavy books. Copy paper works well for leaf rubbing; heavier paper will not.

Say: For the Festival of the Booths, the people were commanded to gather branches as they rejoiced before God. Today, in honor of those branches, let's make leaf rubbings.

Give each child a sheet of paper. Show them how to place a few leaves, not touching, underneath the paper. Rub lightly with a dark crayon as the pattern of the leaves emerges.

Encourage children to admire the patterns. If time permits, give out more paper, then let them rearrange the leaves and do another rubbing or two.

Bonus Activity
Use an appliance box to set up a sukkah for the children to take turns visiting. Give them a simple snack such as an apple slice to bring along with them. If you don't have an appliance box, drape a table with a sheet or blanket.

Saying Goodbye
Give children their sukkot made of cards and their Fall Leaf Rubbings.

Say: The Festival of the Booths is a happy time when people enjoy food and fellowship outdoors in a sukkah. As Christians, we learn about the customs of the Old Testament and celebrate God's blessings.

World Communion Sunday

Message:

Christians all over the world celebrate World Communion Sunday.

Greeting with a Basket

Find an object that represents another country. Cover it with a cloth.

Greet the children. Hold up the basket. Ask a child to remove the cloth and hold up the object or photo. Explain the object or photo to the children.

Say: We're thinking about other places around the world today because we're going to talk about World Communion Sunday. On this Sunday, which is the first Sunday in October, Christians all over the world take Communion. As they do, they think about their Christian brothers and sisters in other parts of the world.

If your children are unfamiliar with Holy Communion and how it is served at your church, give them a bit of information on the sacrament.

Getting Set for the Story

Consider inviting one or several members of your congregation who speak another language to visit Children's Church. At the end of the story, they can teach the children to say some faith words in the language they know.

Telling the Story

Before Jesus ascended into heaven, he said to his disciples: "Therefore, go and make disciples of all nations, baptizing them in the name of the Father and of the Son and of the Holy Spirit." Jesus wanted people all over the world to understand that he was God's son. The disciples did just as Jesus told them. In time, the Christian Church grew. Now there are Christians in every country of the world.

On World Communion Sunday, Christians all over the world take Communion. They use words of our faith, but they sound different because they are spoken in another language. Let's say some of those words today:

In Brazil, they say "peace of Christ" as "paz de Cristo." (paz de Cristo)

In Germany, they say "bread" as "brot." (Brot)

In Italy, they say "cup" as "tazza." (tazza)

In Turkey, they say "Jesus" as "Isa." (Isa)

In the Netherlands, they say "Sunday" as "Zondag." (Zondag)

In Hebrew, they say "love" as "ahava." (ahava)

(Lead the children in saying the English words and the translated words one more time.)

When we hear Christian words spoken in other languages, it helps us understand and be glad there are Christians all over the world.

Bible Verse

Therefore, go and make disciples of all nations, baptizing them in the name of the Father and of the Son and of the Holy Spirit. (Matthew 28:19)

Supplies

- Basket
- Object that represents another country, such as:
  - doll in native dress
  - pottery
  - carving
  - glass
  - embroidery
  - tinwork
  - bracelet
  - necklace
  - postcard
  - magazine photo
- Cloth

Note

The website www.microsofttranslator.com is a good source for translation if there are other words you want to translate for the story.

Pray

God of Our Year, we're glad there are Christians all over the world. Help us to think about them and pray for them, especially on World Communion Sunday. Amen.

Exploring

Decorate Circle the World Plates to remind children there are Christians all over the world.

Make a sample plate. Using a variety of colors, draw a border of stick figure people in a circle around the outside of the plate.

In the center of the circle of people, color a cross. Finally, shade in the rim of the plate with sections of blue and green to represent the land and water on a globe. Attach a length of yarn or ribbon (about 18 inches long) using a hole punch or stapler. Knot at the top to create a hanger.

You may want to precut yarn or ribbon hangers for the children.

Say: When you hang your plate at home, each time you look at it, you'll think of your Christian brothers and sisters around the earth.

Celebrating with Music

Sing songs that celebrate Christians all over the world such as "He's Got the Whole World in His Hands," "Kum Ba Yah," "Jesu, Jesu," and "Jesus Loves the Little Children."

If you have rhythm instruments, this is a fitting time to use them.

More Exploring

Serve children a sampling of international breads. Almost all grocery stores sell a variety of breads such as pita, Hawaiian, rye, French, Italian, matzo, and Irish soda bread. Choose two or more varieties for the children to try. Before Children's Church, cut the bread into sample-size pieces. Keep the bread well wrapped, but plan on serving it in bowls or baskets. The children will appreciate juice or water to go along with the bread.

Say: While he was still on the earth, Jesus served bread and wine to his disciples. Ever since that day, Christians have served bread and wine to remember Jesus. We call this "Holy Communion." Today, in honor of World Communion Sunday, we're going to taste breads from other nations.

Serve the bread and say a few words about each kind.

Bonus Activity

Host an International Festival!

Read picture books set in other countries, show the children folk art or souvenirs from another land, serve international foods, lead the children in a traditional folk dance, and/or play a game that children enjoy in another country. Your local library, the internet, and members of your congregation will be great resources to help with these activities.

Saying Goodbye

Give the children their Circle the World Plates.

Say: In honor of World Communion Sunday, I'm going to say goodbye to you in four languages: *adios,* which is Spanish; *adjø,* which is Norwegian; *hambani kahle,* which is Zulu; and *goodbye,* which is English.

Blessing of the Animals

Message:
We care about God's creatures.

Greeting with a Basket
Place several toy animals in the basket. Cover them with a cloth.

Greet the children. Hold up the basket. Ask a child to remove the cloth and hold up the animals. You may want to have other children help out.

Say: God has filled our world with amazing animals. God wants us to care for the creatures of the earth.

Getting Set for the Story
Read the Bible verse.

Say: Now, let's hear a story about a man who loved God's creatures.

Telling the Story
A long time ago, there lived a man named Francis. Francis was from a wealthy family, but he gave up fancy things to serve God.

Francis loved God's world and the creatures that live in it. Legends say that he talked to birds and wolves, and other creatures too. Legends also say that Francis was the first to create a manger scene, and he used real, live animals! The real animals helped the people of Francis's day understand that Jesus was born in a stable.

Even though Francis lived long ago, he is now considered a saint. In some churches, it has become a tradition to hold a ceremony called a "Blessing of the Animals." These ceremonies are often held in the fall, on or near St. Francis Day, which is October 4.

People bring their pets, from dogs and cats to hamsters and rabbits to birds and snakes, to be blessed. They even bring goldfish in a bowl! Special prayers are said and everyone has a wonderful time admiring the animals. Often these ceremonies are held outside. There's a church in New York City, St. John the Divine, that brings the animals into the church for the ceremony. They've even had camels and kangaroos!

Today, we're going to think about St. Francis and our love for animals as we hold our very own Blessing of the Animals Ceremony.

Exploring
Fashion Creature Puppets for the Blessing of the Animals Ceremony.

Children will use crayons to turn a lunch bag into a paper animal. Consider offering construction paper for creating features such as eyes, ears, nose, whiskers, spots, and tail.

Make a sample Creature Puppet. The bottom flap of the bag is the animal's head and the rest of the bag is the body. Hold up your puppet.

Say: This is a *(type of creature)*, one of God's wonderful creatures. Now you're going to make your own Creature Puppet.

Bible Verse
God said, "Let the earth produce every kind of living thing: livestock, crawling things, and wildlife." (Genesis 1:24)

Supplies
• Toy animals
• Basket
• Cloth

Note
You can find wonderful photos of the event at St. John the Divine and other Blessing of the Animals ceremonies by searching on the internet.

Pray
God of Our Year, thank you for Francis, who loved animals, and thank you for the animals he loved. Help us to do our part to love and care for the animals of your world. Amen.

Supplies

- White or brown paper lunch bags
- Crayons
- Construction paper (optional)
- Scissors (optional)
- Glue or tape (optional)

When the puppets are finished, have the children put them on their hands. Ask them to form a circle or face you in a group.

Say: I am so glad you are here today for our Blessing of the Animals Ceremony. God created amazing animals. Let's all say, "Thanks be to God." *(response)* Owners, now I'm going to ask you each to tell us the name of your animal and the type of animal it is.

Let each child respond.

Say: What a wonderful assortment of creatures we have here today for our Blessing of the Animals Ceremony. Owners, please hold your animals still as we say a prayer.

Pray: Dear God, creator of all creatures, great and small, we ask for your blessing on our puppets because they represent real animals. Thank you for all the creatures you made. Help us to do our best to care for them. Amen.

Celebrating with Music
Say: A favorite Bible story features lots of animals and a man who took care of them! Let's learn a song about Noah and his ark.

Teach children "Who Built the Ark?" by playing a recording or singing the song for them. The words can be found on p. 128.

More Exploring
Celebrate the earth's creatures with a game of Animal Charades.

Put the names of animals on separate note cards or slips of paper. Fold the cards or slips of paper in half and put them in a container. Here are some suggestions for animals: dog, cat, monkey, lion, elephant, giraffe, snake, rabbit, squirrel, fish, duck, alligator, frog, turtle, kangaroo, rhinoceros, bear, cow, horse, sheep, pig, octopus, and dove. Add any others you would like. If you don't want to write down the names of the animals, you can whisper them to the children during the game.

Have the children take turns pulling out animal names. They should first act out the animal without making any sound. If the group can't guess the animal, then the child may make the animal's sound.

Supplies

- Index cards or slips of paper
- Pen or pencil
- Container with wide opening

Bonus Activity
Invite a creature to visit Children's Church along with its owner! Have your guest show the animal to the children.

Saying Goodbye
Give the children their Creature Puppets. Ask them to put the puppet on their hands.

Say: Goodbye, animals! We're glad you could be part of our Blessing of the Animals Ceremony, and glad you get to go home with your new owners.

St. Martin's Day

Message:
God wants us to share with those in need.

Greeting with a Basket
St. Martin's Day, a medieval holiday, is based on the legend of St. Martin, who gave his cape to a beggar shivering with cold. If your basket is too small to hold a jacket, coat, cape, or sweater, place a winter scarf and/or mittens or gloves in the basket. Cover the items with a cloth.

Greet the children. Hold up the basket. Ask a child to remove the cloth and hold up the clothing item.

Say: When we are cold, we are really uncomfortable and unhappy. God wants us to help those in need. One way we can help is to give warm clothes to those who need them.

If your church has a winter clothing or blanket drive, say a word about this now. Explain other ways, too, that your church helps those in need, especially in the winter.

Getting Set for the Story
Say: In the Bible, Jesus says helping someone in need is like helping God. Jesus explains in the story, "When you have done it for one of the least of these brothers and sisters of mine, you have done it for me."

You may want to read all of Matthew 25:31-45.

Ask: What are some ways we can help people who are hungry? Thirsty? Lonely? People who need clothes? People who are sick?

Say: God asks us to share with those in need. Let's hear a story about a man who did just that! It is a legend based on a man who lived a long time ago.

Telling the Story
A long, long time ago, a soldier named Martin was approaching the gate of a city in France. Underneath an archway, he saw a man. The man was huddled against a wall, shivering with cold. The man was poor and hardly had any clothes on. Martin took off his own warm cape. He tore it in half and gave a half cape to the man.

That night, Martin had a dream. In it, Jesus was wearing the cape. Jesus said, "Martin, what you did for the least of my brothers, you did for me."

This dream inspired Martin to quit his life as a soldier. He spent the rest of his days caring for the poor and others who were in need.

After he died, Martin became known as "St. Martin." A holiday called "St. Martin's Day" or "Martinmas" was created in his honor. On November 11, St. Martin's Day was celebrated with lanterns to represent Martin showing God's light to the world. Special foods were served. One of those foods was a croissant or crescent roll in honor of the hooves of Martin's horse and the half of his cape that he gave to the beggar. People don't celebrate St. Martin's Day as much anymore, but today we remember Martin as we think about helping those in need. *(Serve croissants or crescent rolls if you have them.)*

Bible Verse
Then the king will reply to them, "I assure you that when you have done it for one of the least of these brothers and sisters of mine, you have done it for me."
(Matthew 25:40)

Supplies
- Basket
- Cloth
- Coat, jacket, or sweater
- Mittens or scarf (optional)

Supplies
- Croissants or crescent rolls
- Napkins

Pray
God of Our Year, just like St. Martin, help us to share with those in need. Amen.

Supplies

- #4 cone coffee filters
- Plastic drinking straws
- Index cards or cardstock
- Scissors
- Tape or stapler
- Crayons

Supplies

- Two adult-sized coats
- Masking tape

Supplies

- Poster paper
- Markers
- Examples of items to be collected

Exploring

Make St. Martin Puppets. For each puppet, cut a two-inch circle from an index card or card stock for the head.

Give the children a circle. Ask them to give Martin a face. Next give them each a coffee filter. Explain that this is Martin's cape before he tears it and gives it to the beggar. Have them color the cape.

Give each child a straw. Have them poke the straw through the crimped bottom of the coffee filter. Orient the straw so the bottom of the filter is now at the top. Have the children tape or staple Martin's face to the straw. Move the cape up to meet the face and tape or staple it in place.

Celebrating with Music

Teach children "Pass It On" by playing a recording or singing the song for them.

More Exploring

Hold a St. Martin's Coat Relay! Use adult-size coats, but make sure the coats aren't so long that children could trip.

If possible, move to a larger space. Use masking tape to mark off a start/finish line and a turnabout line. Make the lines as far apart as practical.

Say: In honor of Martin and to encourage us to help people who need warm clothes, we're going to have a St. Martin's Coat Relay.

Divide the group into two teams. Position each team behind the start/finish line.

Explain the relay: A player from each team is to put on the coat, walk to the turnabout line, and walk back. This player is to offer the coat to the next person in line, saying, "You look cold. Here's a coat!"

Start the relay by saying the line and offering a coat to the first person on each team.

Bonus Activity

Let your Children's Church kids make posters for an upcoming blanket or clothing drive at church. Bring in examples of the collection items, such as a scarf or socks, so the children will have models to use when creating the posters.

Saying Goodbye

Give children their St. Martin Puppets.

Say: Please show your St. Martin Puppets to everyone you meet as you leave Children's Church today. Tell them about Martin, who offered his cape to a beggar. Martinmas reminds us that God wants us to share with those in need.

All Saints' Day

Message:
We serve God with enthusiasm.

Greeting with a Basket
Find two or more items that represent Christian service at your church and/or in the community. Cover the items with a cloth.

Greet the children. Hold up the basket. Ask a child to remove the cloth and hold up the items. You may want to have other children help out.

Explain how each item relates to church and community service.

Say: As Christians, we are called to serve God with enthusiasm. This means to serve happily with energy and dedication. Today, we're going to talk about a Christian holiday called "All Saints' Day." On this day, we honor those who serve God.

Getting Set for the Story
During the story, children will look at themselves in a mirror. A hand mirror works best, but a makeup compact will do.

Say: When the Christian church was started, the followers wrote letters encouraging one another in their service to God. Here's what Paul said in a letter to the church.

Read the Bible verse.

Say: Paul wanted the early Christians to be enthusiastic as they told others about Jesus and as they worked to form the Christian Church. God wants us to be enthusiastic too! In the Bible, those who work hard for the church are called "saints." Let's talk today about ways that kids can be enthusiastic saints at our church.

Telling the Story
I'm going to ask you some questions. Please answer with enthusiasm!

Should you come to church grumpy or put on a happy face?

Should you keep all your money for yourself or bring some for an offering?

Should you ignore newcomers at church or greet them with a smile?

Should you goof around at the church work day or rake up a pile of leaves?

Should you run in the fellowship hall after church supper or clear the table?

Should you watch hours of TV or help your dad make Thanksgiving pies for the soup kitchen?

Should you keep the ball from a toddler who is crying or play a game of catch with him?

Should you ask for extra candy in the grocery store or help pick out green beans for the canned food collection?

Should you refuse to make get-well cards in Children's Church or color a wonderful picture on the front of yours?

Bible Verse
Don't hesitate to be enthusiastic—be on fire in the Spirit as you serve the Lord! (Romans 12:11)

Supplies
- Basket
- Objects that represent Christian service, such as:
  - a copy of this book or other teaching supplies
  - choir music
  - cans or jars for a food pantry donation
  - gloves or hats for a clothing drive
  - tools that represent upkeep of your church building and grounds
  - anything else that represents service
- Cloth

Supplies
- Mirror

Should you complain when your mom asks you to come with her to visit the nursing home or practice some riddles to tell the people there?

Should you step over litter on the church lawn or pick it up?

Good answers! When we serve God's church with enthusiasm, we are behaving as saints of the church.

(Hold up the mirror.)

Let's each take a look at a saint in honor of All Saints' Day! When the mirror comes to you, look at yourself and then say, "Hi, *(name)*. You're an enthusiastic saint of the church."

(Conclude by looking in the mirror yourself.)

Hi, *(your name)*. You're an enthusiastic saint of the church, and you love serving all the saints here by telling stories in Children's Church!

Exploring

Invite a saint in your congregation to chat with the children. Explain that this week's theme is Christian service. During Children's Church, this guest will talk about his or her Christian faith and his or her service to the church. Along with this, invite your guest to bring a picture book, photographs, childhood toys, mementos, a musical instrument, sports equipment, or hobby items to show the children.

Celebrating with Music

Teach children the refrain to "Here I Am, Lord" by playing a recording or singing the song for them.

Other songs that fit the theme of Christian service include "This Little Light of Mine" and "This Is My Commandment."

More Exploring

Have the children color a portrait of someone they know who serves God with enthusiasm (like your guest speaker).

Encourage the children to think about the guest's presentation and add any embellishments they like to the portrait, such as the guest's gray cat, baseball glove, or teddy bear. Present the portraits to your guest.

Bonus Activity

Your local library should offer picture book biographies of people who served with enthusiasm. Here are a few titles: Barbara Cooney's *Miss Rumphius*, Kathi Appelt's *Miss Lady Bird's Wildflowers*, Doreen Rappaport's *Martin's Big Words*, and Patrick McDonnell's *Me . . . Jane*.

Saying Goodbye

Say: Happy All Saints' Day, saints! Serve God with enthusiasm.

Christ the King Sunday

Message:
God rules over all creation.

Greeting with a Basket
Make a Crown of Faith using the directions in Exploring. Fit the crown to your own head. Put the crown in a basket. (If the finished crown will be too big for your basket, leave one end of the back unconnected and roll it up. You can staple or tape it together during the greeting.) Cover the crown with a cloth.

Greet the children. Hold up the basket. Ask a child to remove the cloth. Then ask the child to hold up the crown.

Put on the crown. (Size it to fit and then put it on, if need be.)

Say: Crowns are worn by kings and queens and other royal figures. Today, we're celebrating Christ the King Sunday. This is the last Sunday in the Christian year. On this day, we honor God as the ruler over all creation.

Getting Set for the Story
Say: Jesus' message was that "God's kingdom has come." On Christ the King Sunday, we celebrate the fact that God rules over all creation through his Son, Jesus the Christ.

During our story, at the end of each line, I'll signal you by putting my hand up in the air. You'll respond by putting your hand in the air too and shouting out, "God rules!"

Telling the Story
God created the world. (God rules!)

God is in charge of the world. (God rules!)

God set the sun and the moon and the stars and the planets in the sky. (God rules!)

God made the oceans and the lakes and the mountains and the deserts and the canyons and the islands. (God rules!)

God made all the creatures of earth and sea and sky. (God rules!)

God knows each and every one of us. (God rules!)

God loves us and hears our prayers. (God rules!)

God gave Jesus, God's son, to the world. (God rules!)

God sent Jesus to teach us about the ways of God. (God rules!)

God wants us to learn from Jesus and pay attention to his teachings. (God rules!)

God sent the Holy Spirit to help and guide us. (God rules!)

God is king of all creation. (God rules!)

(Read the Bible verse to the children. Then divide the verse into sections and have the children say each part after you.)

Bible Verse
Now to the king of the ages, to the immortal, invisible, and only God, may honor and glory be given to him forever and always! Amen.
(1 Timothy 1:17)

Supplies
- Crown (see instructions on page 124)
- Basket
- Cloth
- Stapler or tape (if needed)

Pray
God of Our Year, we're glad you rule over all creation. We pray this prayer in the name of your son, Jesus, who came to teach us about the ways of your kingdom. Amen.

Supplies

- Manila folders (one per child)
- Scissors
- Crayons
- Stick-on gems or foil sticker stars
- Stapler or tape

Supplies

- Instant vanilla pudding
- Fruit cocktail
- Large mixing bowl
- Large spoon
- Cups
- Spoons

Note

Christmas "pudding" resembles a fruitcake more than the modern pudding we usually think of. Traditionally made with raisins, currants, candied fruits, and nuts, it would be mixed on Christ the King Sunday, steamed to cook it, and then hung to dry out or "cure" throughout Advent. Christmas puddings could be stored for up to a year before being eaten.

Supplies

- Index cards
- Ribbon or yarn
- Stapler
- Crayons
- Foil sticker stars (optional)
- Advent stickers (optional)

Exploring

Make Crowns of Faith to celebrate Christ the King Sunday. Prepare the crowns ahead of time. Cut the tabs off the folders. Open the folders and cut each one in half, creating strips approximately 6 x 17 inches. Half of these strips will be crown fronts; the rest are crown backs.

Fold crown fronts in half along the folder's original fold. Cut the points of the crown using a simple zigzag or a more elaborate pattern.

Give each child a crown front and invite them to decorate it using vibrant colors. Offer stick-on gems and/or foil sticker stars.

As children finish, staple or tape one end of a crown back onto one end of the crown front. Size the crown to fit, trimming away some of the crown back if need be. Staple or tape.

Celebrating with Music

Teach the children "He's Got the Whole World in His Hands" by playing a recording or singing the song for them. The words are on p. 128.

More Exploring

Celebrate a holiday of yesteryear, Stir Up Sunday, observed on the last Sunday of the Christian year. This modern version consists of instant pudding and fruit cocktail.

Set out the pudding in a large bowl. Add the fruit cocktail to the pudding.

Say: Advent starts on the Sunday after Christ the King Sunday. Years ago, families made their Christmas pudding on this Sunday. A prayer for this Sunday starts: "Stir up, we beseech thee, O Lord, the wills of thy faithful people," so the day became known as "Stir Up Sunday."

Say: When families made the Christmas pudding, each person took a turn. As they stirred, they made a wish. This is our holiday pudding! You'll each get a turn to stir.

Let each child take a turn stirring the pudding, and then serve it. As the children enjoy the snack, talk about their favorite Christmas foods.

Bonus Activity

Make Advent Streamers to mark the days until Jesus is born. Cut index cards into fourths. Give each child twenty-five note card pieces. Set out foil sticker stars, holiday stickers, and/or crayons. Have children decorate their card pieces. Staple the pieces to a long length of ribbon or yarn. Explain that starting on the first of December, they are to tear off a card piece each day. When all the pieces are gone, it's Christmas!

Saying Goodbye

Ask the children put on their Crowns of Faith.

Say: God is the ruler of creation. On Christ the King Sunday we honor God and God's son, Jesus, who taught us about God's kingdom.

Thanksgiving!

Message:
At Thanksgiving, we thank God for our blessings.

Greeting with a Basket
Look around your home and choose a few items that represent some of the blessings you are thankful for. Consider photos of family and pets, or items that represent a hobby, a food you love, or anything else at all! Put these items in a basket and cover them with a cloth.

Greet the children. Hold up the basket. Ask a child to remove the cloth. Then ask the child to hold up the items one at a time. You may want to have other children help out.

Say: These are some of the blessings I am thankful for. Soon, we'll discuss lots of your blessings, too.

Ask: There's a holiday especially devoted to giving thanks. Can you tell me which one?

Say: God wants us to be thankful every day for our many blessings, but Thanksgiving is an extra special time for giving thanks!

Getting Set for the Story
Say the Bible verse for the children and then lead them in saying it with you.

Say: During our story, which is an ABC story, we're going to shout out praises to God. But first, let's practice our ABC's by singing the alphabet song.

Lead the children in singing the song.

Say: It's good you know your alphabet! The kids in today's story do, too.

Telling the Story
After each line of the story, we're going to shout, "Thanks, God, for" and then we'll fill in the blessing named in the story. Ready?

All the kids in Children's Church were excited about Thanksgiving. In fact they were so excited, that they started shouting out their blessings as fast as they could to the letters of the alphabet.

Jeremy said, "A is for airplanes." Thanks, God, for airplanes!

Seth said, "B is for basketball." Thanks, God, for basketball!

Crystal said, "C is for Christmas." Thanks, God, for Christmas!

Daneka said, "D is for doughnuts." Thanks, God, for doughnuts!

Janie said, "E is for electricity." Thanks, God, for electricity!

Kim said, "F is for Ferris wheel." Thanks, God, for Ferris wheels!

Juan said, "G is for games." Thanks, God, for games!

Tristan said, "H is for helicopters." Thanks, God, for helicopters!

Lizanne said, "I is for igloos." Thanks, God, for igloos!

Finn said, "J is for Jonah and the big fish." Thanks, God, for Jonah and the big fish!

Bible Verse
Let's come before him with thanks! Let's shout songs of joy to him! (Psalm 95:2)

Supplies
- Items you are thankful for
- Basket
- Cloth

Note
You may want to change the names of the children in the story to the names of your Children's Church kids. Names may be repeated.

Caroline said, "K is for kangaroo." Thanks, God, for kangaroos!

Jeremy said, "L is for laughter." Thanks, God, for laughter!

Seth said, "M is for mom." Thanks, God, for moms!

Crystal said, "N is for noses." Thanks, God, for noses!

Daneka said, "O is for ocean." Thanks, God, for oceans!

Janie said, "P is for popcorn." Thanks, God, for popcorn!

Kim said, "Q is for quilts." Thanks, God, for quilts!

Juan said, "R is for row boats." Thanks, God, for row boats!

Tristan said, "S is for seasons." Thanks, God, for seasons!

Lizanne said, "T is for Thanksgiving." Thanks, God, for Thanksgiving!

Finn said, "U is for umbrella." Thanks, God, for umbrellas!

Caroline said, "V is for vacuum cleaners." Thanks, God, for vacuum cleaners!

Jeremy said, "W is for watermelon." Thanks, God, for watermelon!

Seth said, "X is for xylophone." Thanks, God, for xylophones!

Crystal said, "Y is for yogurt." Thanks, God, for yogurt!

Daneka said, "Z is for zoo." Thanks, God, for zoos!

Exploring

Fashion Polka-Dot Horns of Plenty for families to fill at Thanksgiving time.

Horns of Plenty, also known as "cornucopias," are traditionally made from basket material. They are filled with fruits, vegetables, and nuts. If possible, locate a picture of a horn of plenty on a Thanksgiving card or decoration or through an image search on the internet.

Make a sample to show the children. Decorate the bottom side of a paper plate with polka dots. Use a variety of colors and vary the size of the dots. Roll the paper plate into a cone. Staple or tape a few times along the overlapping seam of the cone.

Hold up the picture of a horn of plenty, if you have one.

Say: We see horns of plenty at Thanksgiving time. They are usually filled with fruits, vegetables, and nuts.

Ask: Why do you think these are called "horns of plenty"?

Say: Horns of plenty represent the plentiful blessings we have, especially God's gift of delicious and nutritious foods. We have plenty of good food!

Hold up the sample Polka-Dot Horn of Plenty. Give every child a paper plate and invite them to decorate the bottoms of the plates with colorful polka dots. Tell them to think of one of God's blessings to them as they color each dot. Have the children put their names in the middle of the other side of the plate. Show them how to roll the plates into cone shapes. Staple or tape each horn of plenty.

Say: At home, you can fill your Polka-Dot Horn of Plenty with fruit or other foods for a festive Thanksgiving decoration.

Pray

God of Our Year, thanks for all things good from A to Z! Amen.

Supplies

- Paper plates
- Crayons
- Stapler or tape
- Picture of a horn of plenty (optional)

Celebrating with Music

Teach children "Thank You, God," set to the tune of "Twinkle, Twinkle, Little Star." The song is a familiar grace, with two new lines added.

More Exploring

Celebrate blessings with a game of Thanksgiving Ball!

You can play Thanksgiving Ball on the floor with a large or small ball. If you want to play around a table, a small ball works best.

Say: Thanksgiving is a wonderful holiday! We love the parades, the football games, the delicious foods, the dinner, and spending happy hours with our friends and family. Let's celebrate right now with a game of Thanksgiving Ball!

Have children sit on the floor or around a table. Explain that when it's their turn, they are to call out the name of someone in the circle and then roll the ball to them. That person is to pick up the ball, say the name of something or someone she or he is thankful for, and then roll the ball to another person. (With older children, have them toss the ball if you wish.)

To extend the game, you can play Thanksgiving Ball by calling out categories such as Places, Foods, Friends, Songs, Activities, and Animals. Answers must fit into the designated category.

Bonus Activity

Ice cream cones make delicious horns of plenty. Fill the cones with ice cream, pudding, or yogurt. Place them sideways on individual plates and add fresh or frozen berries or other fruits. Serve with a fork or spoon.

Saying Goodbye

Give children their Polka-Dot Horns of Plenty.

Say: I am so thankful for each of you!

Thank you for the world so sweet,
Thank you for the food we eat,
Thank you for the birds that sing,
Thank you God, for everything,
Thanks all the way from A to Z,
For the blessings you've given me.

Supplies
• Ball

Supplies
• Ice cream cones
• Ice cream, pudding, or yogurt
• Plates
• Berries or other fruits
• Forks or spoons
• Napkins

Who Built the Ark?

(Use with "Blessing of the Animals," p. 118)

Old man Noah built the ark
Built it out of hickory bark.
He built it long, both wide and tall.
Plenty of room for the large and small.

Chorus:
Who built the ark? Noah, Noah.
Who built the ark? Brother Noah built the ark.

Now in came the animals two by two,
Hippopotamus and kangaroo.
Now in came the animals three by three,
Two big cats and a bumblebee. (Chorus)

In came the animals four by four
Two through the window and two through the door.
In came the animals five by five,
The bees came swarming from the hive. (Chorus)

Well, here came the animals six by six,
The elephant laughing at the monkey's tricks.
In came the animals seven by seven,
Giraffes and camels looking up to heaven. (Chorus)

In came the animals eight by eight,
Some were on time but the others were late.
In came the animals nine by nine,
Some were laughing and some were crying. (Chorus)

In came the animals ten by ten,
Time for the voyage to begin.
Noah said, "Go shut that door,
The rain's started falling and we can't take more."
(Chorus)

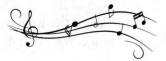

He's Got the Whole World In His Hands

(Use with "Christ the King Sunday," p. 124)

He's got the whole world in his hands,
He's got the whole world in his hands,
He's got the whole world in his hands,
He's got the whole world in his hands.

He's got the itty bitty baby in his hands . . .

He's got you and me, brother, in his hands . . .

He's got you and me, sister, in his hands . . .

He's got everybody here in his hands . . .

He's got the wind and the rain in his hands . . .

He's got the sun and the moon in his hands . . .

He's got the whole world in his hands . . .